101 Foundations for the UNSTOPPABLE Christian Young Athlete

101 Life-Shaping PRINCIPLES for Athletes to Build RESILIENCE and CONFIDENCE, and Lead With FAITH and CHARACTER.

FROM: _______________

TO: _______________

DATE: _______________

NOTE: _______________

TABLE OF CONTENTS

PART 4: RISE ABOVE FAILURE LIKE MANNY PACQUIAO

PART 5: CHOOSE SECRET INTEGRITY LIKE AARON JUDGE

PART 6: LEAD

WANT TO REMEMBER THE VERSES? OR TEST YOURSELF WHENEVER YOU WANT ON YOUR PHONE AND KNOW WHICH VERSE MEANS WHAT?

» **TRAIN YOUR MIND LIKE YOUR BODY**: master verses anytime with 50 fun, game-ready flashcards on

» **INSTANT CONFIDENCE**: hints + scripture help you remember what each verse means, fast.

» **PARENTS INCLUDED**: 20 bonus cards to coach, quiz, and grow together

» **SCAN THIS QR CODE AND GET ACCESS TODAY!**

Stop navigating the high-pressure, toxic sports and school culture alone.

Join a our community of Christian parents dedicated to building rooted reens who are even stronger in their faith.

What's Inside the Community:

» Safe Community: Connect with parents who value character over the scoreboard.

» Use the map to connect to other Christian parents close to you who also bought our books and joined.

» Get all of our next books sent to you for free as an advanced reviewer.

» Custom Worship Song: A professional anthem featuring your teens name & scripture of your choice ($250 Value!)

» Recruiting & Scholarship Kit: Clear steps to the next level without the stress.

» More bonuses and materials will be added!

Scan the QR code to Join us.

BEFORE THE WHISTLE BLOWS

You're standing on the sideline. **Heart pounding. Palms sweating.** The coach is about to call your name, and that voice inside your head starts whispering again.

 "What if I mess up? What if everyone watches me fail? What if I'm just not good enough?"

God already answered that question. He said you are **fearful and wonderfully made.** He said He has **plans to prosper you and not to harm you.** He said He did **not give you a spirit of fear, but of power, love, and a sound mind.** The Creator of the universe looked at you and called you **enough before you ever stepped on a field.**

But knowing that and feeling that in the heat of competition are two very different things. And you're not the only one who has struggled with that gap.

> » **Lionel Messi,** the greatest soccer player who ever lived, felt that exact same fear as a tiny, sick kid in Argentina that no club wanted to pay for.

> » **Steph Curry** heard it when every major college told him he was too short and too skinny.

> » **Giannis Antetokounmpo** heard it while selling sunglasses on the streets of Athens just to eat dinner.

> » **Simone Biles** heard it so loud on the Olympic stage that she had to step back entirely before she could step forward into greatness again.

> » **Manny Pacquiao** heard it while sleeping on the streets of the Philippines at 14 years old with nothing but his fists and a prayer.

Every single one of them became unstoppable Not because the voice disappeared. Not because the odds changed.

Because they **anchored their identity in God first** and let their sport flow from that foundation.

They learned what to do with the doubt, the pressure, and the pain.

That is exactly what this book gives you.

Not motivational fluff you forget by tomorrow..

Not generic advice from people who never competed.

101 real foundations, each one built from the true story of a world-class athlete who walked through the exact same fire you're walking through right now.

> » Performance anxiety that makes your hands shake.

> » Slumps that make you want to quit.

> » Coaches who don't play you.

> » Teammates who don't pass to you.

> » Parents who push too hard or don't understand.

> » The comparison trap that eats you alive every time you open your phone.

> » The loneliness of feeling like you're the only one struggling while everyone else looks fine.

You're not the only one.

Science proves it.

> » Over **60% of young athletes deal with performance anxiety.**

> » Research shows **negative self-talk can steal up to 30% of your actual ability.**

> » Athletes whose entire identity is wrapped in their sport are **twice as likely to crash into depression after a setback.**

These are real numbers from real studies, and this book addresses every single one of them with **real solutions, not lectures.**

Here is what makes this different from anything else on your shelf. Every chapter gives you:

> » **a story that hits**

> » **a scripture that sticks**

> » **a scientific insight that clicks**

> » **a practice you can start today**

» Not next month. **Today.** In under two minutes of reading.

And here is the ground rule, the one truth this entire book is built on.

Your sport is what you do. It is never who you are.

You are a child of God who happens to compete. Your worth was settled at the cross, not at the scoreboard. When you build your life on that foundation, you become the kind of athlete that no loss can destroy and no win can inflate. You become unstoppable, not because of talent, but because of who you are.

This book is for every young athlete between 10 and 16 who has ever felt **not enough**. It is also for the parent sitting in the bleachers wondering how to help without pushing too hard. **You are both welcome here.** There is no shame in these pages. Only growth.

One more thing. You do not have to read all 101 foundations in order. You can, and the book is built to flow that way. But :

   » if you are in a slump right now, flip to Part 4.

   » If anxiety is choking your game, go straight to Part 8.

   » If your team chemistry is broken, Part 7 is waiting.

   » If you just need to hear that God has not forgotten you, start with Part 2.

   » **Wherever you start, start today.**

The whistle is about to blow.

Read it your way. Front to back like a devotional, or flip straight to the chapter that matches your struggle today. **Both work perfectly.**

One chapter a day. Each foundation takes about two minutes to read. Do one every morning before school or practice. In 101 days, you will be **a completely different competitor.**

Say the prayer out loud. It is only one sentence. But speaking it changes something inside you that reading silently never will.

Do the practice. Every chapter ends with one specific action. Not homework. A challenge. Do it before bed that night.

Share it.

> » Text a chapter to a teammate who needs it.

> » Read one out loud with your family at dinner.

> » Bring it to the locker room.

> » These foundations spread best when they are **lived out loud, not kept quiet on a shelf.**

Write in it.

> » Circle the scriptures that hit hardest.

> » Underline the sentences that feel like they were written about you.

> » Dog-ear the pages you need to revisit.

> » A Christ-centered athlete's book should look **well-loved, not brand new.**

Parents, you belong here too. You can read alongside your athlete. Let the chapters start conversations instead of arguments. Ask them which foundation hit them hardest today. Then listen. **That is it.**

PRAISE

Terrence M., 8th Grader and AAU Basketball Player

*I do not read books much but my sister told me to try this and I read five foundations the first night because I kept saying just one more. The resilience one hit me because **my family cannot afford trainers or camps like other players**. It showed me how to **build strength from what I lack instead of complaining**. I started **treating every limitation as training**. Our narrow hallway became my ball handling gym and rebounding my own shots built more conditioning than anyone on my team. My AAU coach said **I look like a completely different player in tight games**. I used to **shut down late when we were losing** and now I get **leader loud**. The character foundation changed how I carry myself because I learned **real confidence is staying locked in when things go wrong**. I read one every morning before school and **this book made me feel like not having everything is my superpower**. If you feel behind get this book because it will change how you see everything.*

Marcus T., Father of a 14 Year Old Soccer Player

*My son **wanted to quit after being pulled at halftime** and replaced by a player who scored twice. I gave him this book and he read twelve foundations in one night. The next morning he taped a resilience quote to his mirror about getting back up fast and **something shifted**. He **stopped spiraling after mistakes** and started leading warmups. I can see **the difference in how he carries himself**. The confidence foundations finally reached him in a way I could not. The faith foundations opened conversations about God and identity we had struggled to start. Now we read one together driving to practice and **it is the best part of my week. He is not the same kid who wanted to quit**. If your child is struggling with confidence or thinking about quitting their sport get this book because **it does the heavy lifting without making teens feel lectured**.*

Brianna K., High School Junior and Varsity Volleyball Player

*The character leadership foundation **broke something open in me** because I thought leadership meant being loud or having stats. This book showed me leadership is **how you respond when things go wrong and treat people when nobody watches**. I started encouraging younger teammates and my coach said **our practice energy completely changed**. The confidence foundations fixed my game because I used to **replay mistakes and spiral**. Now I **reset fast** because **my identity is not built on my last play**. The faith foundations feel real and one made me cry because it described exactly what I feel before matches and walked me through surrendering it. I read one every night and **this book is turning me into someone I respect on and off the court**. If you are* *a female athlete who gets in her head **get this immediately.***

Pastor Mike S., Youth Pastor and Chaplain

*Team chapels usually **lose attention in minutes** but **this book solved that.** Each foundation is short and vivid enough that athletes lean in. When I read a resilience one at football chapel **the room shifted** and a linebacker said it described his whole season. The theology is solid yet natural and connects scripture to real athlete struggles so well kids absorb verses without realizing. The character foundations sparked **deep talks about integrity that sermons never reached.** A two minute foundation **met them where they are.** If you work with young athletes in ministry **this is the resource you have been waiting for** because all 101 foundations land and I now use it weekly.*

Rebecca D., Mother of a 15 Year Old Swimmer

*My daughter **hit a mental wall,** plateaued, and **cried before meets. This book changed everything.** The resilience foundations taught her a plateau means rebuild with intention and she asked her coach to return to fundamentals. **Her times dropped within weeks.** The confidence foundations stopped the pre-meet crying because she learned **her worth is not attached to times.** She now **feels free in the water again.** The faith foundations created conversations about God, identity, and purpose we had struggled to start and she now texts me reflections. She even wrote **I am brave and God is with me** on her goggles case. The character foundations show at home too because she is kinder and more patient. Buy this for your child and read it yourself because **you will both be changed.***

Coach Vanessa R., Head Varsity Girls Basketball Coach

*In fourteen years of coaching, **nothing has changed my team culture like this book.** My players **lead, encourage louder, and handle adversity with composure.** It builds **identity, confidence, and character together.** I now use a foundation every practice and **see lasting growth in every athlete.***

BEFORE THE WHISTLE BLOWS

You're standing on the sideline. Heart pounding. Palms sweating. The coach is about to call your name, and that voice inside your head starts whispering again. "What if I mess up? What if everyone watches me fail? What if I'm just not good enough?"

God already answered that question. He said you are fearful and wonderfully made. He said He has plans to prosper you and not to harm you. He said He did not give you a spirit of fear, but of power, love, and a sound mind. The Creator of the universe looked at you and called you enough before you ever stepped on a field.

But knowing that and feeling that in the heat of competition are two very different things. And you're not the only one who has struggled with that gap.

Lionel Messi, the greatest soccer player who ever lived, felt that exact same fear as a tiny, sick kid in Argentina that no club wanted to pay for. Steph Curry heard it when every major college told him he was too short and too skinny. Giannis Antetokounmpo heard it while selling sunglasses on the streets of Athens just to eat dinner. Simone Biles heard it so loud on the Olympic stage that she had to step back entirely before she could step forward into greatness again. Manny Pacquiao heard it while sleeping on the streets of the Philippines at 14 years old with nothing but his fists and a prayer.

Every single one of them became unstoppable. Not because the voice disappeared. Not because the odds changed. Because they anchored their identity in God first and let their sport flow from that foundation. They learned what to do with the doubt, the pressure, and the pain.

That is exactly what this book gives you.

Not motivational fluff you forget by tomorrow. Not generic advice from people who never competed. 101 real foundations, each one built from the true story of a world-class athlete who walked through the exact same fire you're walking through right now. Performance anxiety that makes your hands shake. Slumps that make you want to quit. Coaches who don't play you. Teammates who don't pass to you. Parents who push too hard or don't understand. The comparison trap that eats you alive every time you open your phone. The loneliness of feeling like you're the only one struggling while everyone else looks fine.

You're not the only one. Science proves it. Over 60% of young athletes deal with performance anxiety. Research shows negative self-talk can steal up to 30% of your actual ability. Athletes whose entire identity is wrapped in their sport are twice as likely to crash into depression after a setback. These are real numbers from real studies, and this book addresses every single one of them with real solutions, not lectures.

Here is what makes this different from anything else on your shelf. Every chapter gives you a story that hits, a scripture that sticks, a scientific insight that clicks, and a practice you can start today. Not next month. Today. In under two minutes of reading.

And here is the ground rule, the one truth this entire book is built on.

Your sport is what you do. It is never who you are.

You are a child of God who happens to compete. Your worth was settled at the cross, not at the scoreboard. When you build your life on that foundation, you become the kind of athlete that no loss can destroy and no win can inflate. You become unstoppable, not because of talent, but because of who you are.

This book is for every young athlete between 10 and 16 who has ever felt not enough. It is also for the parent sitting in the bleachers wondering how to help without pushing too hard. You are both welcome here. There is no shame in these pages. Only growth.

One more thing. You do not have to read all 101 foundations in order. You can, and the book is built to flow that way. But if you are in a slump right now, flip to Part 4. If anxiety is choking your game, go straight to Part 8. If your team chemistry is broken, Part 7 is waiting. If you just need to hear that God has not forgotten you, start with Part 2.

Wherever you start, start today.

The whistle is about to blow.

Read it your way. Front to back like a devotional, or flip straight to the chapter that matches your struggle today. Both work perfectly.

One chapter a day. Each foundation takes about two minutes to read. Do one every morning before school or practice. In 101 days, you will be a completely different competitor.

Say the prayer out loud. It is only one sentence. But speaking it changes something inside you that reading silently never will.

Do the practice. Every chapter ends with one specific action. Not homework. A challenge. Do it before bed that night.

Share it. Text a chapter to a teammate who needs it. Read one out loud with your family at dinner. Bring it to the locker room. These foundations spread best when they are lived out loud, not kept quiet on a shelf.

Write in it. Circle the scriptures that hit hardest. Underline the sentences that feel like they were written about you. Dog-ear the pages you need to revisit. A Christ-centered athlete's book should look well-loved, not brand new.

Parents, you belong here too. You can Read alongside your athlete. Let the chapters start conversations instead of arguments. Ask them which foundation hit them hardest today. Then listen. That is it.

PART 1: BEYOND THE GAME
LIKE TIM TEBOW

1
IDENTITY BEYOND THE GAME

"And we know that in all things God works for the good of those who love Him." Romans 8:28

Tim Tebow stood on the biggest stage in college football, hoisting the Heisman Trophy while cameras flashed like a thousand suns. He led Florida to two national championships. Everyone said he was destined for NFL greatness. Then team after team cut him. Commentators laughed on live TV, calling him "finished." But here is what shook people: Tebow never broke. Not once. He did not spiral into anger or vanish into silence. Why? Because football was never his identity. God was.

Scientists in the Journal of Sport & Exercise Psychology found athletes who build their whole identity around their sport are twice as likely to face depression after setbacks. Tebow already knew this truth. He picked up a baseball bat, started a foundation for kids with special needs, and kept shining. His worth was settled before any game began. So when you lose a match and that voice whispers "you are nothing without this sport," remember: you are a child of God first, an athlete second. That order changes everything.

Prayer

Lord, remind me daily that my worth lives in You, never on any scoreboard. Amen.

Practice

Write "I am God's child first" on your wrist tape or water bottle. Read it before every practice this week.

2

HEART OVER HIGHLIGHT REELS

"The Lord does not look at the things people look at. People look at the outward appearance, but the Lord looks at the heart." 1 Samuel 16:7

Everyone wanted Tim Tebow's stats. Scouts measured his arm angle, his throwing motion, his forty yard dash. They picked him apart on TV like he was a science experiment. Some analysts said his mechanics were ugly. But here is what those scouts missed completely: locker rooms changed when Tebow walked in. Teammates played harder. Injured players felt seen. He visited sick children in hospitals before every single college game, quietly, with no cameras, sometimes holding a kid's hand for an hour. No stat sheet tracked that.

Research from Harvard's Human Flourishing Program shows that character driven leaders elevate entire team performance by up to 33%. God was never checking Tebow's throwing spiral. He was watching how Tebow treated the backup quarterback nobody noticed. Your coach might post stats on the wall. Your followers might count your highlights. But God is scrolling through something deeper: your heart. The kid who encourages a struggling teammate after a brutal loss already has the stat that matters most. That one never expires.

Prayer

God, shape my heart before my highlights. Let my character speak louder than any stat. Amen.

Practice

Before your next game, quietly encourage the teammate who gets the least attention. Do it with zero audience.

3

FIRST THINGS FIRST

"But seek first His kingdom and His righteousness, and all these things will be given to you as well." Matthew 6:33

Sunday mornings were sacred for Tim Tebow. Even during the chaos of NFL training camps, early morning meetings, and grueling football schedules, he made church and faith community non negotiable. Some people thought it was extreme. Teammates sometimes questioned it. But Tebow understood something most young athletes miss: if you fill your week with only sport, your spirit slowly empties. He kept God first, and everything else found its place around that center.

Studies from the University of North Texas found that athletes who maintain faith and community involvement outside sport report 40% higher life satisfaction and longer careers. Here is the real talk: nobody is saying skip practice for youth group. But if your entire week is just train, compete, scroll, sleep, repeat, you are running on fumes and calling it dedication. Block time for God the same way you block time for drills. Put it on the schedule. Protect it fiercely. When your spirit is full, your game does not shrink. It grows. Seeking God first is not losing time. It is multiplying it.

Prayer

Father, help me put You first even when my schedule screams there is no room. Amen.

Practice

Set one recurring alarm this week labeled "God First." Use those ten minutes for prayer or scripture before training.

4

LEGACY OVER TROPHIES

"For I know the plans I have for you, declares the Lord, plans to prosper you and not to harm you, plans to give you hope and a future." Jeremiah 29:11

When Tim Tebow got released from professional football, reporters shoved microphones in his face, expecting bitterness. Instead, he smiled and talked about his foundation. The Tim Tebow Foundation had already hosted "Night to Shine" proms for over 100,000 people with special needs across 50 countries. Trophies collect dust on shelves. But thousands of kids spinning under disco lights in crowns, feeling loved for the first time? That legacy breathes and grows forever. Tebow played the long game with his life, not just his career.

Psychologists call this "future self continuity," and research from UCLA shows teens who vividly picture their future selves make significantly better daily decisions. So ask yourself the legacy question right now: when your sport is over, and it will be over someday, what will people remember? Not your scoring average. They will remember how you made them feel. They will remember your kindness in the hallway, your patience with the younger kid at camp, your faith when things got hard. Start building that legacy today. Every small, good choice is a brick in something eternal.

Prayer

God, give me eyes to see beyond today's game and build something that outlasts every season. Amen.

Practice

Write down one sentence answering: "What do I want people to say about me in 20 years?" Tape it to your mirror.

5

WINNING WITHOUT BRAGGING

"Let someone else praise you, and not your own mouth; an outsider, and not your own lips." Proverbs 27:2

After Tim Tebow threw four touchdowns and led a miracle comeback against Cincinnati in the NFL playoffs, the world exploded. "Tebow Time" trended everywhere. Reporters begged for his reaction. He could have pounded his chest and declared himself the greatest. Instead, cameras captured him deflecting every compliment to his teammates, his coaches, and God. He literally kneeled in gratitude on the field. That image became so iconic it got its own word: "Tebowing." He won the biggest moment and made it about everyone else.

Neuroscience from Wake Forest University reveals that humility after success actually increases dopamine and trust within teams, making future wins more likely. Here is the trap: you score the winning goal, hit the clutch shot, or finish first, and the spotlight feels incredible. Your chest swells. You want to let the whole world know. But the athletes people respect forever are the ones who shine and then point the light somewhere else. Stay grounded. Thank your teammates. Thank God. The win already spoke for you. You never have to announce your own greatness when your character is doing it silently.

Prayer

Lord, when I win, keep my heart humble. Let my gratitude be louder than my ego. Amen.

Practice

After your next big moment, publicly credit a teammate or coach before saying anything about yourself.

6

WHEN THE DOOR SLAMS SHUT

"The Lord is close to the brokenhearted and saves those who are crushed in spirit." Psalm 34:18

The phone call came. Then another. Then silence. Tim Tebow was cut from the New England Patriots, then the Philadelphia Eagles, then the New York Jets. Three NFL teams said, "You are not good enough." Imagine chasing your dream your entire life, winning everything in college football, and then hearing "no" over and over from professionals. Tebow later admitted those nights were painful, lonely, and confusing. But he never questioned God's love. He just kept showing up.

Research from the American Psychological Association confirms that rejection activates the same brain regions as physical pain. Getting cut literally hurts. So if you have ever been dropped from a team, lost your starting spot, or watched someone else take your position, that ache in your chest is real and valid. But here is what Tebow learned: a closed door is not a closed life. God was not punishing him. God was redirecting him toward something bigger than football could ever be. Your worst rejection might be your greatest redirection. Sit with the pain. Let God hold you in it. Then get back up.

Prayer

Father, when doors close and my heart breaks, remind me You are closer than ever. Amen.

Practice

Write down one rejection you have faced. Beside it, write one good thing that came after. See the pattern.

7

YOUR PERSONAL MISSION STATEMENT

"Where there is no vision, the people perish." Proverbs 29:18

Before Tim Tebow ever played a snap of college football, he already knew his mission: use every platform God gave him to bring faith, hope, and love to people who need it most. That clarity guided every decision. When the NFL said no, his mission did not die because his mission was never "play football forever." It was bigger. That personal vision statement carried him through professional baseball tryouts, book deals, TV broadcasting, and building a global foundation. Vision kept him moving when circumstances tried to stop him.

Sports psychologists at the University of Virginia found that athletes with a clear personal mission statement show 37% more resilience during setbacks than those without one. Most teens drift through seasons without ever asking "why am I doing this?" That is how burnout sneaks in. You train, compete, and grind but for what? Grab a notebook tonight and write it down. Not just sport goals like "make varsity." Go deeper. "I compete to glorify God and inspire others through my effort." That is a mission. When you know your why, no loss can steal your direction.

Prayer

God, give me a vision for my life that is bigger than any single game or season. Amen.

Practice

Write a one sentence personal mission statement tonight. Read it out loud every morning before school this week.

8

BOLD, NOT COCKY

"Do nothing out of selfish ambition or vain conceit. Rather, in humility value others above yourselves." Philippians 2:3

There is a famous clip of Tim Tebow in the college football national championship halftime. Florida was losing. The cameras zoomed in on his face, and what the world saw was pure, quiet fire. Not trash talk. Not panic. Not arrogance. Just steady, unshakeable belief. He told his teammates, "We are going to give everything we have." Florida came back and won. That was confidence: a calm knowing rooted in preparation and faith. Cockiness screams "look at me." Confidence whispers "watch what God does through us."

Researchers at the University of Melbourne found that athletes who display humble confidence are rated as better leaders and receive more support from teammates than those who boast. Here is the honest difference: cockiness needs an audience. Confidence does not care who is watching. Cocky athletes crumble when they fail because their identity was built on everyone else's applause. Confident athletes recover because their foundation goes deeper than any crowd. You can believe fully in your abilities without belittling anyone else. Train like a beast. Compete with everything you have. Then let your work speak and your humility echo.

Prayer

Lord, fill me with quiet, unshakeable confidence rooted in You, never in my own pride. Amen.

Practice

Catch yourself this week. Every time you want to boast, compliment a competitor or teammate instead.

Your feedback is a true blessing!

If this book has encouraged you or helped you feel less alone, would you leave a quick review?

Even one sentence makes a huge difference and takes just a minute. As a small author, your feedback not only lifts my heart... it also helps other children of God find the support and hope they need.

Thank you for being part of this journey!

Scan this QR code with your phone to go to the review page and find this book.

Or

Go to your orders, find the book and click

"Write a product review"

Thank you <3

PART 2: PLAY FOR GOD ALONE LIKE STEPH CURRY

9

AUDIENCE OF ONE

"Whatever you do, work at it with all your heart, as working for the Lord."
Colossians 3:23

The arena roars with 20,000 voices, but Steph Curry kneels quietly in the tunnel, scribbling "I Can Do All Things" on his sneakers. Nobody sees it. No camera catches the ink. That message is between him and God. The skinny kid from Charlotte that Virginia Tech rejected, that his own dad's college turned away, now plays basketball for an audience of One.

Curry does not perform for highlight reels or Twitter mentions. Every crossover, every three pointer, every sprint back on defense is an offering. When reporters ask about four NBA championships, he shrugs and says, "It's all God." Research from the Journal of Sport Behavior found athletes who play for internal purpose over external approval show 31% more consistency under pressure. You feel that pressure too. The parents watching. The coach analyzing. The scouts judging. But when you decide the only eyes that truly matter are God's, something wild happens. The anxiety drops. The joy returns. You stop performing and start playing free. That is the secret Curry found at tiny Davidson College, and it carried him to greatness.

Prayer

Lord, remind me I play for You alone. Your approval is all I need. Amen.

Practice

Before your next game, write a short scripture on your wristband, shoe, or tape. Let it anchor you to your true audience.

10
SPORT AS WORSHIP

"Offer your bodies as a living sacrifice, holy and pleasing to God; this is your true and proper worship." Romans 12:1

Watch Steph Curry during a random Tuesday practice in November. No crowd. No cameras. No trophy on the line. He still launches 500 shots. Still sprints every drill. Still dives for loose balls like it is Game 7. Why? Because for Curry, effort is not about impressing coaches. It is worship. Every bead of sweat is a thank you to the God who gave him legs that run, lungs that breathe, and hands that shoot.

Most people think worship only happens on Sunday mornings with music and prayers. But Romans 12:1 flips that completely. Your body, pushed to its max, is a living sacrifice. That brutal conditioning session? Worship. That extra rep when your muscles scream? Worship. Sport science confirms that athletes who attach deeper meaning to training sustain motivation 40% longer than those chasing only wins. So tomorrow when practice feels pointless, remember this: God gave you your body as a gift. Using it fully, joyfully, and honestly is the loudest worship you will ever offer. You do not need a stage. The court, the field, the pool is your altar.

Prayer

God, let every rep, every sprint, and every practice be my worship to You. Amen.

Practice

At your next practice, pick the hardest drill and give 100% effort, silently dedicating it to God as your offering.

11
PRAY WITHOUT CEASING

"Pray without ceasing." 1 Thessalonians 5:17

Fourth quarter. Finals. Steph Curry stands at the free throw line with the game hanging by a thread. Millions watching. Palms sweating. But before he bounces the ball, his lips move slightly. Not trash talk. Not a breathing exercise. Prayer. Curry has talked openly about praying before games in the locker room, during timeouts on the bench, and after losses in the shower. Prayer is not his emergency button. It is his constant conversation.

Most teens think prayer needs a quiet room, closed eyes, and five uninterrupted minutes. That is one way. But "pray without ceasing" means something bigger. It means a two second whisper before a sprint. A silent "help me, God" when nerves hit during warmups. A quick "thank You" after a good play. A 2020 study in Psychology of Religion and Spirituality found faith-anchored athletes experienced 34% lower competitive anxiety because they were not carrying the weight alone. You were never meant to carry it alone. Prayer is not a ritual. It is a lifeline. Talk to God like He is right beside you, because He literally is. On the bus. In the locker room. Mid-game. Always.

Prayer

God, teach me to talk to You constantly, in wins, in losses, in everything between. Amen.

Practice

Set three prayer triggers today: before practice starts, during a water break, and after you finish. Keep each one under ten seconds.

12

THE GOSPEL LENS ON LOSING

"Consider it pure joy, my brothers and sisters, whenever you face trials of many kinds, because you know that the testing of your faith produces perseverance." James 1:2-3

In 2016, Steph Curry's Golden State Warriors blew a 3-1 lead in the NBA Finals. The greatest regular season in basketball history ended in heartbreak. Cameras zoomed in on Curry's face. Tears. Silence. The whole world expected him to crumble. Instead, he came back the next season and won the championship. When asked how he survived that loss, Curry pointed to his faith: "God does not promise easy. He promises purpose." Here is the lie that quietly destroys young athletes: "If God loves me, He will let me win." That is not faith. That is a vending machine. Real faith says, "God is growing me through this." James 1:2-3 does not say losing feels good. It says losing produces perseverance, and perseverance builds something inside you that winning alone never could. Studies confirm that athletes who process defeat through a growth lens recover emotionally 47% faster than those who see loss as failure. So when you lose, and you will, do not ask "Why me, God?" Ask "What are You building in me?" That question changes everything. Losses are not punishments. They are sculpting tools in the hands of a God who is making you unstoppable.

Prayer

Father, when I lose, help me trust that You are building something greater inside me. Amen.

Practice

After your next tough loss, write down one specific thing it taught you. Keep a "Growth from Losses" note on your phone.

13

SCRIPTURE FOR GAME DAY

"I can do all things through Christ who strengthens me." Philippians 4:13

Every single game. Every single shoe. "I Can Do All Things." Steph Curry has written Philippians 4:13 so many times that the verse is practically tattooed into his pregame routine. But here is what most people miss: that verse is not about guaranteed victory. Paul wrote it from a prison cell. It means "I can endure anything, good or bad, because Christ holds me." Curry gets that. The verse is his anchor, not his lucky charm.

Your brain under pressure is like a browser with 50 tabs open. Fear, doubt, comparison, all running at once. Scripture closes those tabs. Neuroscience research shows that repeating a meaningful phrase before high stress moments activates the prefrontal cortex, the part of your brain responsible for calm focus and decision making. That is not magic. That is how God designed your mind. Find your anchor verse. Maybe it is Joshua 1:9, "Be strong and courageous." Maybe it is Isaiah 41:10, "Fear not, for I am with you." Write it down. Memorize it. Repeat it in warmups, at the starting line, in the huddle. When panic screams, let scripture whisper louder. Curry did not become the greatest shooter alive on talent alone. He built his mind on the Word.

Prayer

Lord, plant Your Word deep in my heart so it steadies me when pressure hits. Amen.

Practice

Choose one scripture verse this week. Write it somewhere you will see it daily. Repeat it five times before every practice and game.

14
GRATITUDE BEFORE EVERY WHISTLE

"This is the day that the Lord has made; let us rejoice and be glad in it."
Psalm 118:24

Before the opening tip, Steph Curry does something most fans miss. He looks up. Not at the scoreboard. Not at the opponent. Up. A small, quick glance toward the ceiling, a silent acknowledgment that this moment, this game, this healthy body, is a gift. The kid who was told he was too small to play major college basketball now stands on the biggest stages in sports, and he never forgets who gave him the chance.

Gratitude is not just a nice feeling. It is a competitive weapon. Research from UC Davis found that grateful athletes reported 25% higher energy levels and significantly better sleep before competitions. Why? Because gratitude rewires your brain away from anxiety and toward appreciation. When you step onto the field worried about messing up, your body tightens. When you step on grateful just to be there, your body relaxes and performs freely. Tomorrow before the whistle blows, pause for three seconds. Think: "I get to do this. Not everyone can. Thank You, God." That tiny shift from "I have to" to "I get to" changes your entire game. Gratitude is not weakness. It is the fuel of champions.

Prayer

God, before I compete, remind me that every game is a gift from You. Amen.

Practice

Before your next game, stand still for five seconds during warmups and silently name three things you are grateful for.

15

THE WITNESS ON THE FIELD

"Let your light shine before others, that they may see your good deeds and glorify your Father in heaven." Matthew 5:16

After a brutal loss in the 2019 NBA Finals, Steph Curry did something that shocked millions. Instead of storming off the court, he walked to the opposing team's bench and personally congratulated every single player. Cameras captured him hugging opponents, smiling through obvious pain. Social media exploded. Not because of a highlight dunk or a record broken, but because of how he handled defeat. That moment preached louder than any sermon.   People are watching you. Not just your coach, not just your parents. Your teammates. Your opponents. The younger kids in the stands who want to be you someday. They are studying how you react when the ref makes a bad call, when you get benched, when you lose by one point. Behavioral research shows that emotional reactions during competition are the single biggest factor in how teammates evaluate a leader's character. You are a walking sermon every time you compete. You do not need to quote Bible verses on the field. Just respond to adversity with grace, and people will ask where your peace comes from. That question is the open door. Your character under pressure is your loudest testimony.

Prayer

Lord, let how I act when things go wrong point others straight to You. Amen.

Practice

After your next tough moment in a game, choose one calm, respectful response instead of reacting emotionally. Notice how others respond to you.

16

GOD'S TIMING, NOT YOURS

"There is a time for everything, and a season for every activity under the heavens." Ecclesiastes 3:1

Steph Curry waited. And waited. And waited. No major college scholarship. Three years at a school most basketball fans had never heard of. He was not drafted first overall. Not second. Not fifth. He went seventh, and scouts still questioned whether his skinny frame could survive the NBA. It took six professional seasons before he won his first championship. Six years of people doubting, questioning, and underestimating him. God's clock was not broken. It was perfectly set.

You feel it right now. The teammate who got the starting spot you deserved. The growth spurt that has not come yet. The scholarship offer that went to someone else. It burns. Developmental research shows that athletes who peak later often sustain longer, healthier careers because their foundation is deeper. God is not ignoring your prayers. He is building your roots before He grows your branches. Curry's delay was not denial. It was preparation. Every overlooked year at Davidson sharpened his shooting, toughened his mind, and deepened his faith. Your waiting season is doing the same thing for you right now, even if you cannot see it yet. Trust the timing. Your moment is coming.

Prayer

Father, give me patience to trust Your timeline even when mine feels too slow. Amen.

Practice

Write down one thing you are waiting for in your sport. Below it, write one skill you can sharpen while you wait. Start today.

PART 3: CONQUER YOUR MIND LIKE GIANNIS ANTETOKOUNMPO

17
CATCH IT, CHANGE IT

"For God has not given us a spirit of fear, but of power, love, and a sound mind." 2 Timothy 1:7

A skinny teenager in Athens, Greece shares one pair of basketball shoes with his brother. They take turns at practice. Giannis Antetokounmpo spent mornings selling sunglasses on dusty streets so his family could eat dinner. Every voice around him said the same thing: too thin, too raw, too poor. When the NBA drafted him, analysts called it a wasted pick. But the loudest critic was never the analysts. It was the voice inside his own head whispering, "You don't belong here."

Giannis learned to catch that whisper mid-sentence. Queen's University research shows unmanaged negative self-talk drops performance by 30%. That means your inner critic literally steals a third of your talent. Giannis did a self-talk audit: catch the lie ("I'm not enough"), challenge it ("Says who?"), and change it ("God gave me power, love, and a sound mind"). He became a two-time MVP and NBA champion. Your brain fires over 6,000 thoughts daily. You do not have to believe every single one.

Breakthrough Insight: The voice in your head is not always telling the truth. You have permission to argue back.

Prayer

Lord, help me recognize lies in my thinking and replace them with Your truth. Amen.

Practice

Write down one negative thought you had today. Cross it out. Write the opposite truth beside it. Repeat daily.

18

I CAN'T DO THIS YET

"Being confident of this, that He who began a good work in you will carry it on to completion until the day of Christ Jesus." Philippians 1:6

Giannis Antetokounmpo's first NBA season was rough. He could barely shoot. His ball handling was shaky. Highlight reels from 2013 show a kid who looked completely lost against grown men. Sports commentators laughed. Social media roasted him. But Giannis never once said, "I can't do this." He said something way more powerful: "I can't do this yet." That tiny three-letter word changed everything. He spent hours in empty gyms, rebuilding his jumper, strengthening his frame, trusting the process God started in him.

Scientists call this a growth mindset. Stanford psychologist Carol Dweck proved that athletes who add "yet" to their failures improve significantly faster than those who accept defeat as permanent. Giannis went from a raw prospect to the most dominant basketball player on the planet. After winning the 2021 championship, he thanked God for the talent and the journey. Philippians 1:6 was alive in him. God started the work. God will finish it. Your struggle today is not your story's ending. It is just an unfinished chapter.

Breakthrough Insight: "Yet" is the most powerful word in your vocabulary. Use it every time you feel stuck.

Prayer

God, remind me that You are not finished with me. My struggle is not my ending. Amen.

Practice

Every time you say "I can't," force yourself to add "yet" out loud. Do this for seven straight days and watch your confidence shift.

19
ESCAPE THE COMPARISON TRAP

"Each one should test their own actions. Then they can take pride in themselves alone, without comparing themselves to someone else." Galatians 6:4

Before Giannis became a global superstar, he shared a court with players who had elite trainers, fancy gear, and years of polished technique. He had none of that. Imagine standing next to someone who looks like they were born for this while you are still figuring out footwork. The temptation to compare was constant. But Giannis focused on one thing only: Am I better than yesterday's version of me? Not better than the kid across the gym. Just better than himself twenty-four hours ago.

Comparison is a thief that never gets full. It always wants more of your joy. Psychologists at the University of Michigan found that social comparison increases anxiety and decreases motivation in young athletes. Giannis understood something deep: God gave him his own lane. His own timeline. His own gift. When you measure your chapter three against someone else's chapter twenty, you will always feel behind. But Galatians 6:4 says test your own actions. Run your race. Nobody else's shoes fit your feet anyway.

Prayer

Father, free me from comparing my journey to anyone else's. My lane is enough. Amen.

Practice

Pick one skill you are improving. Track only YOUR progress this week. No looking at anyone else's stats or highlights.

20

SHOULDERS BACK, EYES UP

"Have I not commanded you? Be strong and courageous. Do not be afraid; do not be discouraged, for the Lord your God will be with you wherever you go." Joshua 1:9

Watch any clip of Giannis Antetokounmpo walking onto a basketball court. Before he touches a ball, before the whistle blows, his presence speaks. Shoulders pulled back. Chin lifted. Eyes locked forward like he already knows what is about to happen. This was not always natural. As a teenager in Athens selling goods on the street, Giannis often walked with his head down, hoping nobody noticed him. But somewhere between poverty and greatness, he learned that confidence starts in the body before it reaches the brain. Harvard social psychologist Amy Cuddy proved that "power posing" for just two minutes increases confidence hormones by 20%. Your body literally tells your brain how to feel. When you slouch, your mind whispers defeat. When you stand tall, your mind prepares for battle. Giannis chose courage physically before he ever felt it emotionally. Joshua 1:9 is not a suggestion. It is a command: be strong and courageous. God walks with you into every gym, every field, every moment that scares you. So lift your chin. He is already there.

Prayer

God, help me carry myself with the courage You already placed inside me. Amen.

Practice

Before your next practice or game, stand tall for two minutes. Shoulders back, chin up, deep breaths. Let your body set the tone.

21
RECRUITER-PROOF YOUR FEED

"Above all else, guard your heart, for everything you do flows from it."
Proverbs 4:23

Giannis Antetokounmpo became famous fast. Millions of followers. Constant attention. Every post scrutinized. But even before the fame, Giannis understood something most young athletes miss: what you put online becomes your permanent resume. Coaches, scouts, recruiters, and future teammates will scroll your feed before they ever watch your game film. Giannis kept his social media clean, positive, and God-centered. He posted workouts, family moments, and gratitude. No drama. No reckless rants. His digital footprint matched his character.

Research from Kaplan Test Prep shows that 35% of college admissions officers have checked applicants' social media, and what they found has cost students their spots. One angry post. One thoughtless video. Gone. Proverbs 4:23 says guard your heart because everything flows from it. Your feed is a window into your heart. If it is full of negativity, gossip, or foolishness, that is what people will assume about you. Giannis protected his name the same way he protected the basketball. Fiercely and intentionally. Your future self will thank you for every post you decided not to upload.

Prayer

Lord, give me wisdom to protect my name and my heart in every space, online and off. Amen.

Practice

Scroll your last twenty posts right now. Delete anything a coach, teacher, or future teammate would question. Start fresh today.

22

THE GRANDMA RULE

"Be very careful, then, how you live, not as unwise but as wise, making the most of every opportunity." Ephesians 5:15-16

Giannis Antetokounmpo grew up deeply connected to his family. His mother Veronica sacrificed everything for her boys. Every decision Giannis made publicly, he filtered through one question: would this make my family proud? That simple filter kept him grounded when fame could have pulled him sideways. In interviews, he credits his mother's values for keeping him wise when the world offered every distraction imaginable. He never posted anything online that would embarrass the people who believed in him first.

This is the Grandma Rule. Before you post, comment, or share anything, ask yourself: would my grandma, my mom, or my pastor smile if they saw this? If the answer is no, do not hit send. Ephesians 5:15 says live wisely and make the most of every opportunity. Every post is an opportunity. To inspire. To encourage. To represent your faith. Or to waste it on something foolish that disappears in seconds but damages trust for years. Giannis chose wisely at every turn. You have that exact same choice sitting in your hand right now.

Breakthrough Insight: If it would make the people who love you most cringe, it does not deserve your name on it.

Prayer

God, give me a filter that honors You and the people who sacrifice for me daily. Amen.

Practice

Before posting anything this week, pause and ask: "Would Grandma approve?" If you hesitate even slightly, delete it.

23
STOP NEGATIVITY

"Walk with the wise and become wise, for a companion of fools suffers harm." Proverbs 13:20

Growing up in Athens, Giannis Antetokounmpo had to choose carefully who he spent time with. Some kids on the streets were headed nowhere good. Giannis could have followed. Instead, he gravitated toward his brothers and people who pushed him toward something better. When he reached the NBA, the same principle applied. He surrounded himself with teammates, coaches, and mentors who made him sharper. He quietly distanced himself from voices that drained his focus, both in person and on his phone screen.

Your environment shapes your mindset more than your willpower ever will. Research from the University of Notre Dame shows that you absorb the attitudes of the five people you interact with most. That includes the accounts you follow online. If your feed is full of people tearing others down, flexing fake lifestyles, or spreading negativity, that poison seeps into your thinking without you even noticing. Proverbs 13:20 is clear: walk with the wise and you become wise. Giannis curated his circle with the same discipline he brought to training. Your unfollow button is one of the most powerful tools you own.

Breakthrough Insight: You become what you consume. Protect your mind like you protect your body before a big game.

Prayer

Father, show me who builds me up and who tears me down. Give me courage to choose wisely. Amen.

Practice

Unfollow three accounts today that make you feel anxious, jealous, or negative. Replace them with three that inspire and encourage you.

24
BUILD A WIN FILE

"I will remember the deeds of the Lord; yes, I will remember your miracles of long ago." Psalm 77:11

After Giannis Antetokounmpo won the 2021 NBA Championship, reporters asked if he ever imagined this moment. He paused. Then he talked about selling trinkets on the streets of Athens, about sharing shoes with his brother, about nights when dinner was not guaranteed. Giannis kept those memories close. Not to stay in pain, but to remind himself how far God had brought him. Every struggle was proof that quitting would have been the wrong choice. His past became fuel, not a prison.

You need an encouragement file. A note on your phone where you save every compliment a coach gives you, every personal record you break, every kind text from a teammate. On bad days, and they will come, you open that file and remember: you have been good before, and you will be good again. Psalm 77:11 says remember God's deeds. Your encouragement file is a collection of evidence that God has been working in your life all along. Giannis never forgot where he started. That is exactly why he appreciated where he ended up.

Breakthrough Insight: On your worst days, your encouragement file will remind you of what your emotions are trying to make you forget.

Prayer

Lord, help me collect and remember every sign of Your faithfulness in my journey. Amen.

Practice

Start a note on your phone called "Proof I'm Growing." Add one win, compliment, or answered prayer to it today. Keep building it.

25

"I GET TO" CHANGES EVERYTHING

"Serve the Lord with gladness; come before His presence with singing."
Psalm 100:2

It is 5:30 AM. The alarm screams. Practice in an hour. Your legs ache from yesterday. Your brain groans, "I have to go train." Now imagine Giannis Antetokounmpo as a teenager in Athens. No gym membership. No proper court. No guarantee he would even be allowed to stay in Greece because his family lacked citizenship papers. He would have given anything for the alarm clock you are cursing at. Every practice, every drill, every sprint you complain about is a gift someone somewhere is praying for.

Gratitude rewires the brain. Neuroscientists at UCLA found that practicing gratitude activates the hypothalamus, reducing stress and boosting motivation measurably. When Giannis finally got his chance in the NBA, he never said "I have to train." He said "I get to." That shift turned obligation into worship. Psalm 100:2 says serve the Lord with gladness. Your sport is a form of service. Your body is a gift. Your opportunity is not a burden. Giannis remembered the streets of Athens every single morning. Let that perspective transform your next early alarm from a groan into a thank you.

Prayer

God, forgive me for complaining about things others are praying for. I get to do this. Amen.

Practice

Tomorrow morning, before your feet hit the floor, say out loud: "I get to train today." Do this every morning for one week.

26

"NEXT PLAY"

"Forget the former things; do not dwell on the past. See, I am doing a new thing!" Isaiah 43:18-19

Round four. Manny Pacquiao's legs buckle. A brutal right hook from Juan Manuel Marquez sends him crashing face first into the canvas. Cameras flash. The arena gasps. Millions watching think it is over. But here is what most people never saw. In the locker room afterward, Manny did not replay that punch a thousand times. He prayed, stood up, and said five words that changed everything: "We prepare for the next fight." No spiral. No shame loop. Just forward. That knockout could have ended his career. Instead, Pacquiao came back and won his next bout because he refused to let one terrible moment define him. Neuroscientists at the University of Chicago found that athletes who mentally "release" mistakes within seconds perform 31% better in the next sequence. You miss the shot. You drop the pass. Your brain screams "REPLAY" like a broken video on loop.   But God literally tells you to forget the former things. Not because the mistake does not matter, but because the next play matters more. Manny learned this from scripture before he learned it from boxing. When he gave his life to Christ, he stopped living in regret about his broken past and started living in what God was doing right now. You can do that too. Not tomorrow. Right now. The next drill, the next rep, the next play. That is your only job.   Breakthrough Insight: Champions do not have fewer failures. They just have shorter memories. Release the last play. God is already doing something new.

Prayer

Lord, free my mind from replaying mistakes. Help me trust your next thing. Amen.

Practice

After every mistake in practice this week, whisper "next play" and physically reset your posture before the next rep.

PART 4: RISE ABOVE FAILURE LIKE MANNY PACQUIAO

27

LOSSES ARE USEFUL

"Listen to advice and accept discipline, and at the end you will be counted among the wise." Proverbs 19:20

Fourteen year old Manny Pacquiao was sleeping in cardboard shelters on the streets of Manila, fighting in unsanctioned boxing matches just to afford rice. He lost fights early on. Badly. But even as a hungry kid with no coach and no plan, Manny did something brilliant after every loss. He never asked "why me?" He asked "what can I fix?" When he finally found a real trainer, Freddie Roach noticed this immediately. Manny did not make excuses. He did not blame the referee. He walked in, sat down, and asked, "What did I do wrong? Show me." Roach later said that single habit is what separated Pacquiao from thousands of equally talented fighters who never made it. "Why" questions trap you. "Why did I play so bad?" leads to spiraling, self-pity, and zero solutions. But "what" questions unlock growth. "What happened on that play?" "What can I adjust?" Research in the Journal of Applied Sport Psychology confirmed that athletes using "what" based reflection improved skill correction rates by 40% compared to those stuck in "why" loops. God's word says accept discipline and you will become wise. Discipline is not punishment. It is information. Every loss is talking to you. Stop asking why it happened. Start asking what it is teaching you. Breakthrough Insight: Losses are not your enemy. Staying confused about them is. Ask "what," get answers, grow wise.

Prayer

God, give me the courage to ask honest questions and the humility to hear the answers. Amen.

Practice

After your next tough game, write three "what" questions: What went well? What broke down? What will I drill tomorrow?

28
RESILIENCE MUSCLE

"We also glory in our sufferings, because we know that suffering produces perseverance; perseverance, character; and character, hope." Romans 5:3-4

November 2012. Manny Pacquiao lay unconscious on the canvas in Las Vegas. Knocked out cold by Marquez in the sixth round. Reporters wrote his career obituary. Fans said he was finished. But Manny had survived worse. He had survived hunger as a child. He had survived living on streets where kids disappeared. He had survived the emptiness of fame without faith. So a knockout? That was just another rep in the gym of resilience. Within weeks, Pacquiao was training again. Within months, he was winning again. The British Journal of Sports Medicine confirmed what Manny lived: resilience, not raw talent, is the single strongest predictor of long-term athletic success.   Resilience is not something you are born with. It is built. Like a muscle. Every hard practice where you want to quit but finish anyway, every bad game you show up after, every embarrassing moment you survive, you are literally building neural pathways that make you tougher. Romans 5 maps it out perfectly: suffering builds perseverance, perseverance builds character, character builds hope. It is a chain reaction. Manny discovered this after giving his life to Christ. He stopped seeing knockdowns as endings and started seeing them as God's training program. Your bad game last week? That was not a disaster. That was a rep.

Breakthrough Insight: You are not falling apart. You are being built. Every hard moment is adding steel to your soul.

Prayer

Father, help me see struggle as training, not punishment. Build resilience in me. Amen.

Practice

This week, when something hard hits, say out loud: "This is building me." Track three moments where you chose to push through.

29

THE "3" QUESTIONS

"Let us examine our ways and test them, and let us return to the Lord."
Lamentations 3:40

After Manny Pacquiao gave his life to Christ, something shifted in how he handled competition. Before faith, a loss would send him into days of silence, partying, avoidance. After faith, he developed a reflection practice that his trainers noticed immediately. Win or lose, Pacquiao would sit quietly after every fight and ask himself three honest questions. His coaching team eventually built this into their formal process because the results were undeniable. Manny stopped repeating the same mistakes. He evolved faster than fighters half his age. He became the only boxer in history to win world titles across eight weight divisions, and he credits this habit of ruthless self-examination as much as any physical training.

Here are the three questions you can steal right now. One: What did I do well today? Start with truth, not trash talk against yourself. Two: What broke down? Be specific, not dramatic. Not "everything was terrible" but "my footwork slipped in the second half." Three: What is one thing I will work on tomorrow? Just one. Lamentations 3:40 says examine your ways and return to the Lord. That means honest inventory plus handing it to God. Sport psychologists call this "structured reflection," and studies show it accelerates improvement by up to 23%. Most athletes skip this. They either avoid the film or drown in self-criticism. You are going to be different.

Prayer

God, give me eyes to see truth about my performance and grace to keep growing. Amen.

Practice

After every practice or game, journal answers to these three questions before you do anything else. Make it habit.

30
BREAK SLUMPS

"Let us not become weary in doing good, for at the proper time we will reap a harvest if we do not give up." Galatians 6:9

There were stretches in Manny Pacquiao's career where nothing clicked. Between 2012 and 2014, he lost two major fights and drew another. Pundits declared him washed up. Fans moved on. Sponsorships dried up. It felt like the universe was screaming "quit." But Manny had learned something powerful after becoming a Christian. He stopped obsessing over results and started trusting the process. Every single morning: Bible reading, prayer, then training. Not glamorous. Not viral. Just showing up. His trainer Freddie Roach said during that slump, Manny actually trained harder than during his championship years. He focused on the daily reps, not the distant trophy. And then, in 2015, the harvest came. He defeated Chris Algieri, then Brandon Rios, and stormed back to the top of boxing.

Slumps lie to you. They whisper that your hard work is pointless, that you have lost "it" forever. But science disagrees. Research in performance psychology shows that outcome focused thinking during slumps increases anxiety by 37%, while process focused thinking, concentrating only on controllable daily actions, is the fastest exit. Galatians 6:9 is literally God's anti-slump prescription: do not grow weary. At the proper time, you will reap. Not maybe. Will. Manny believed that with his whole heart during his darkest boxing years. The harvest has a schedule you cannot see. Your only job is to keep planting.

Prayer

Lord, when results disappear, anchor me to the process. My harvest is coming. Amen.

Practice

Write down three daily controllable actions for your sport. Focus only on those this week. Ignore the scoreboard completely.

31
RESULTS FOLLOW

"For the revelation awaits an appointed time; it speaks of the end and will not prove false. Though it linger, wait for it; it will certainly come." Habakkuk 2:3

For years before his comeback, Manny Pacquiao prayed every single morning. He read scripture. He trained with absolute discipline. And still, the wins did not come. People around him questioned everything. "Maybe God does not care about your boxing career, Manny." "Maybe you should just retire." It would have been so easy to agree. But Pacquiao held onto something fiercer than any punch he ever threw: faith in God's timing. He told reporters during that dry season, "God gave me another chance. I will not waste it." He was not talking about boxing. He was talking about his life. And when the victories finally returned, they carried a weight and a joy that his earlier, faithless championships never had.   This is the hardest foundation in this entire book. Doing everything right and seeing nothing change. You train. You pray. You eat clean. You show up early. And you still sit on the bench. You still lose. You still get overlooked. Habakkuk 2:3 was written for exactly this moment. The promise has an appointed time. It will not prove false. Though it lingers, wait for it. Research from the Journal of Sport and Exercise Psychology found that athletes with high "delay of gratification" capacity outperform peers over five year spans, even when early results were identical. God is not slow. He is strategic. Your season is being prepared.

Prayer

God, when I cannot see progress, help me trust your timeline over my feelings. Amen.

Practice

Write Habakkuk 2:3 on a card. Read it before every practice this week, especially on days you feel invisible.

32

THE 24-HOUR RULE

"Weeping may stay for the night, but rejoicing comes in the morning." Psalm 30:5

December 8, 2012. The worst night of Manny Pacquiao's career. Lying flat on the canvas, completely unconscious. When he woke up, confusion. Then the slow, crushing wave of reality. He had been knocked out in front of the entire world. That night, Manny wept. He sat in his hotel room with his wife Jinkee and he let the pain hit him fully. He did not pretend it was fine. He did not post a motivational quote. He grieved. But here is the part that made Manny a true champion: the next morning, he prayed, ate breakfast with his family, and began planning his return. He gave himself permission to feel every ounce of that loss, but he put a deadline on the darkness. Twenty four hours. Feel it. Then fix it.

Too many young athletes do one of two extremes. They either stuff the pain down and pretend they are fine, which builds invisible pressure until they explode. Or they marinate in it for weeks, replaying the failure until it becomes their identity. The 24-hour rule gives you a healthy middle path. Sport psychologists at the Australian Institute of Sport formally recommend this approach, finding that athletes who process emotions within a bounded timeframe recover motivation 35% faster. Psalm 30:5 knew this thousands of years before any study. Weeping stays for the night. But morning comes. God built sunrise into the system for a reason. Let the night be heavy. Then let the morning be new.

Prayer

Lord, let me grieve honestly tonight and wake up ready to rebuild tomorrow. Amen.

Practice

After your next tough loss, allow yourself to feel it fully until bedtime. Then next morning, write one action step forward.

33
SETBACK TO STORY

"You intended to harm me, but God intended it for good, to accomplish what is now being done, the saving of many lives." Genesis 50:20

Nobody would have scripted Manny Pacquiao's life as a success story. Born in brutal poverty. A sixth grade dropout. Homeless at fourteen. Exploited by promoters. Knocked out on global television. His marriage nearly destroyed by gambling and emptiness. Every chapter of his early story read like a setup for failure. But after surrendering his life to Christ, Manny began to see his entire painful history differently. Those streets taught him hunger. Those early losses taught him adjustment. That emptiness taught him that trophies cannot fill a soul. Pacquiao went on to win titles in eight weight classes, serve in the Philippine Senate, and build schools and hospitals across his country. Every setback i a setup.

This is not toxic positivity. This is not pretending bad things are secretly good while they are crushing you. This is looking back, after the storm passes, and realizing God recycled your pain into purpose. Genesis 50:20 is one of the most powerful verses in the Bible because Joseph said it to the very brothers who sold him into slavery. They meant it for harm. God meant it for good. Research from post-traumatic growth studies shows that 70% of people who endure significant adversity report finding unexpected meaning and strength afterward. Your worst moment is not your final chapter. It is raw material. God is not finished writing your story. The setback you are sitting in right now? One day, it will be the most powerful part of your testimony.

Prayer

God, take my worst moments and turn them into my most powerful testimony. Amen.

Practice

Write down your biggest setback. Below it, write one way it could become a strength. Pray over it daily.

PART 5: CHOOSE SECRET INTEGRITY LIKE AARON JUDGE

34
INTEGRITY WHEN NOBODY SEES

"Whoever walks in integrity walks securely, but whoever takes crooked paths will be found out." Proverbs 10:9

The 2022 baseball season. Yankee Stadium shaking. Aaron Judge rounds the bases after home run number 62, breaking the American League record. But here is what made the moment legendary. In an era where previous record holders got caught using steroids, Judge did it clean. Zero shortcuts. Zero suspicion. Every rep earned, every swing honest. When the whole sport questioned whether big numbers meant dirty play, Judge answered with a crystal clear conscience.

Growing up adopted, Judge could have carried bitterness or felt like he had something to prove through any means necessary. Instead, he carried quiet strength. He once told reporters, "My faith is the foundation. I know who I'm playing for." Research from the Josephson Institute found 72% of teen athletes act unsportsmanlike when nobody is watching. That statistic is your invitation to be different. When you skip a rep because coach turned away, or copy homework because nobody checks, you are withdrawing from yourself. Judge proved that the person who never cuts corners never has to look over their shoulder. Integrity is not a disadvantage. It is your unfair advantage.

Prayer

Lord, make me the same person in secret that I am in public. Amen.

Practice

Pick one area you have been cutting corners in this week. Do it fully and honestly today, even if nobody notices.

35

RESIST THE SHORTCUT

"No temptation has overtaken you except what is common to mankind. And God is faithful; He will not let you be tempted beyond what you can bear." 1 Corinthians 10:13

The party invite. The group chat with the answers. The supplement a teammate swears will make you faster. Aaron Judge faced baseball's biggest temptation. Performance enhancing drugs were everywhere. Players around him bulked up suspiciously, chased records with chemical help, and some got away with it for years. Judge watched all of it and chose the harder road. Clean training, honest reps, slower progress. When he finally broke that record, nobody could whisper "but did he really earn it?"

You face your own version every week. Maybe it is not steroids, but it is the vape at a teammate's house, copying a test, or faking an injury to skip conditioning. The pull feels impossible in the moment. But Paul's words in Corinthians are not motivational fluff. They are a promise. God will always give you a way out. Every single time. Judge found his exit door through faith and discipline. Your exit door might be one honest "nah, I'm good" away. The thing about shortcuts is they always lead somewhere longer and uglier than the original path.

Prayer

God, when temptation feels bigger than me, remind me You are bigger still. Amen.

Practice

Identify your number one temptation this season. Write down your "exit sentence," the exact words you will say when the moment comes.

36

KEEP THEIR NAME SAFE

"A perverse person stirs up conflict, and a gossip separates close friends."
Proverbs 16:28

After games, Aaron Judge's teammates consistently said the same thing about him. He never talks behind anyone's back. In a Yankees clubhouse full of massive egos and constant media pressure, Judge became the teammate everyone trusted. Not because he was the biggest or the best, but because players knew their name was safe in his mouth. When reporters tried to bait him into criticizing struggling teammates, Judge redirected every time. "We are all in this together."

Think about your locker room. How fast does gossip travel? One comment about a teammate's bad game, whispered to two people, becomes a whole squad divided by Tuesday. Science backs this up. Research on team cohesion shows gossip is the single fastest destroyer of trust in group settings. Here is the real test. It is easy to say nice things about someone standing next to you. The measure of your character is what you say about them when they are not in the room. If Judge, playing under the brightest spotlight in sports, could protect his teammates' names, you can protect your friend's reputation in a group chat.

Prayer

Lord, let my words build people up, especially when they cannot hear me. Amen.

Practice

For one full week, say absolutely nothing about a teammate unless you would say it directly to their face.

37
WIN WITHOUT CRUSHING

"Do not gloat when your enemy falls; when they stumble, do not let your heart rejoice." Proverbs 24:17

Home run 62. History made. Cameras everywhere. The losing pitcher had just surrendered the most famous hit of the season, and every eye in the stadium locked onto Aaron Judge. What did he do? He ran the bases with joy but not arrogance. He did not stare down the pitcher. He did not taunt. He tipped his helmet, hugged his teammates, and acknowledged the moment with gratitude instead of ego. Pure class under maximum spotlight.

You know the feeling. You score the game winner, you beat the kid who talked trash all week, and something inside you wants to let them hear it. But Proverbs 24:17 is brutally direct. God does not want you celebrating someone else's pain. Winning with humility is not being soft. It is being strong enough to not need validation from someone else's embarrassment. Studies on athlete behavior show that gloating actually increases opponents' motivation against you in future matchups. So trash talk after a win literally hurts your future performance. Judge understood this instinctively. Greatness does not need to announce itself. The scoreboard already did.

Prayer

Father, let my victories honor You and never humiliate others. Amen.

Practice

After your next win, find one opponent, shake their hand, and say something genuinely respectful about their effort.

38

LOSE WITHOUT EXCUSES

"Humble yourselves, therefore, under God's mighty hand, that He may lift you up in due time." 1 Peter 5:6

The 2022 ALCS. Aaron Judge and the Yankees lost to the Astros. After a record breaking regular season, it ended with a painful playoff exit. Reporters surrounded Judge's locker, microphones out, waiting for him to blame umpires, complain about calls, or point fingers at teammates who struggled. He did none of it. Judge looked into the cameras and simply said the Astros played better. No excuses. No deflection. Just honest, humble ownership of a brutal loss.

Losing already stings. Adding excuses on top does not ease the pain. It just delays growth. When you say "the ref was trash" or "I was tired" or "my teammate messed up," you hand your power to something outside yourself. You become a victim instead of a student. Peter's instruction to humble yourself is not about feeling small. It is about trusting that God sees the full picture even when you are stuck staring at a scoreboard that went the wrong way. Neuroscience confirms that athletes who accept losses without blame recover faster and perform better in their next competition. Judge got right back to work that offseason. Humility is not weakness. It is rocket fuel.

Prayer

God, teach me to lose with the same character I want to win with. Amen.

Practice

After your next tough loss, write down one honest thing you could have done better. No blame, just ownership.

39
RESPECT THE REF

"Let everyone be subject to the governing authorities, for there is no authority except that which God has established." Romans 13:1

Bad calls happen. Aaron Judge knows. In a 162 game baseball season, umpires miss pitches, blow calls, and sometimes change the outcome of entire at bats. But Judge built a reputation for something rare in professional sports. He almost never argues with umpires. While other players scream, throw helmets, and get ejected, Judge steps back, takes a breath, and gets ready for the next pitch. He treats officials like human beings doing a difficult job, not enemies.

You have probably had a ref make a terrible call against you. Your whole body floods with anger. That is normal. But Romans 13:1 flips the script. Authority figures, even imperfect ones, serve a purpose in God's design. Research on youth sports shows that athletes who consistently argue with officials experience higher stress hormones and lower focus in the minutes following an outburst. You literally play worse after yelling at a ref. Judge figured this out. Respect is not agreement. You can disagree with a call and still control your response. The ref controls the whistle. You control your character. One of those matters way more long term.

Prayer

Lord, help me respect authority even when decisions feel unfair. Amen.

Practice

Next game, no matter what call is made, respond with zero complaint. Just reset and play the next moment.

40
TELL THE TRUTH

"The Lord detests lying lips, but He delights in people who are trustworthy."
Proverbs 12:22

Aaron Judge keeps it honest. When coaches ask how his body feels, he tells them. When his parents check in, he does not perform fake toughness. In interviews, Judge has talked about how his adoptive parents built honesty into his foundation from childhood. "They never hid anything from me," Judge said about learning he was adopted. "That honesty gave me freedom." That freedom became the bedrock of a career built on transparency, no hidden motives, no image games, no saying one thing and doing another.

Lying to coaches and parents feels easy in the moment. "Yeah, my shoulder feels fine." "No, I did not miss any reps." "Practice was great." Small lies seem harmless. But Proverbs 12:22 does not rank lies by size. God detests all of them equally. Research on adolescent development shows that teens who habitually lie to authority figures experience significantly higher anxiety levels because maintaining false stories requires constant mental energy. You are literally exhausting your brain keeping track of fake versions of reality. Honesty might sting for five seconds, but it frees you permanently. Judge plays free because he lives honest. Tell your coach the truth. Tell your parents the truth. Watch how light you feel.

Prayer

Father, give me courage to be honest even when the truth is uncomfortable. Amen.

Practice

Today, tell your coach or parent one honest thing you have been holding back, even if it is small.

41
OWN IT OUT LOUD

"Whoever conceals their sins does not prosper, but the one who confesses and renounces them finds mercy." Proverbs 28:13

Early in his career, Aaron Judge went through brutal slumps. Strikeouts piling up, fans questioning everything. Some athletes hide behind excuses or blame mechanics, the weather, anything external. Judge walked to the microphone and said it plainly. "I'm not getting it done. I need to be better." No spin. No hiding. Public ownership of his failures. And every single time he said it, something shifted. Teammates rallied. Coaches respected him more. The slump broke.

Admitting mistakes publicly feels like standing in a freezing rainstorm with no jacket. Every part of you screams "protect yourself." But Proverbs 28:13 promises that concealing failure blocks your progress, while confessing it opens the door to mercy. Psychology research confirms this. Studies on accountability show that publicly owning mistakes increases trust from peers by over 40% and accelerates personal improvement. When you tell your team "I messed up that play, my fault," something powerful happens. You take the weight off everyone else. You become someone people want to follow. Hiding mistakes makes them grow. Owning them makes them shrink. Be like Judge. Step up and say it.

Prayer

God, give me the bravery to own my mistakes and the humility to grow from them. Amen.

Practice

Next time you make an error in practice or a game, say "my bad" immediately and out loud. No waiting.

42

GUARD YOUR NAME DAILY

"A good name is more desirable than great riches; to be esteemed is better than silver or gold." Proverbs 22:1

Aaron Judge's reputation was not built in one moment. It was built in thousands of invisible ones. The way he treated bat boys in the dugout. The way he stayed after games to sign autographs for kids. The way he never posted disrespectful content online. Every single interaction was a deposit into what you could call his "reputation bank." By the time he broke that home run record, his name carried weight that no contract could buy.

Your reputation works the same way. Every choice, from how you talk to younger players to what you post on social media to whether you return the equipment cart without being asked, is either a deposit or a withdrawal. Proverbs 22:1 says your name is worth more than money. Think about that. More than any trophy, any scholarship, any ranking. Research on character perception shows it takes roughly twenty positive interactions to build trust and only one negative moment to shatter it. That ratio is not fair, but it is real. Judge understood that your name walks into rooms before you do. Build it so carefully that when people hear it, they think of someone worth respecting.

Prayer

Lord, help me make deposits into my reputation every single day through my actions. Amen.

Practice

Ask yourself tonight: "Did my actions today add to or subtract from my name?" Write down one specific deposit you made.

43

LEAD WITHOUT THE TITLE

"Don't let anyone look down on you because you are young, but set an example for the believers in speech, in conduct, in love, in faith, and in purity." 1 Timothy 4:12

Every NFL scout said the same thing: "Too short." At 5'11", Russell Wilson heard it from draft analysts, coaches, even fans who thought an undersized quarterback could never survive the league. But Wilson never waited for permission to lead. At the University of Wisconsin, before he was named captain, before anyone handed him authority, he was the first player in the weight room and the last voice encouraging teammates after brutal losses. He led with his feet, his habits, and his presence. No armband required.

Here is the truth that changes everything: leadership is not a position. It is a pattern. Research from the Institute for Applied Positive Psychology shows that informal leaders, those without titles, often influence team culture more than captains do. You do not need your coach to announce your name. You need to be the one who picks up the cones, who stays late, who never rolls their eyes during drills. When Paul wrote to young Timothy, he was saying exactly this: your age is irrelevant if your example is undeniable. That quiet kid who always works hard? Everyone notices. Be that kid.

Prayer

Lord, help me lead through what I do, not what I am called. Amen.

Practice

Tomorrow, be first to every drill and last to leave. Do it without announcing it to anyone.

PART 6: LEAD WITH IMPACT LIKE RUSSELL WILSON

44

SAY EXACTLY WHAT YOU MEAN

"Therefore encourage one another and build each other up, just as in fact you are doing." 1 Thessalonians 5:11

After Russell Wilson threw one of the most heartbreaking interceptions in Super Bowl history, costing Seattle the championship, his locker room could have fractured. Blame could have spread like poison. But Wilson did something unusual in the days that followed. He did not offer hollow "good job" statements to teammates. He pulled guys aside individually and told them exactly what they contributed. Specific plays. Specific moments. "You held that block on third down that gave us the drive in the second quarter." That level of detail told each player: I actually see you.

A University of Michigan study found teams with a 5 to 1 ratio of positive to negative communication outperform peers by 31%. But here is the key: generic praise does almost nothing. "Nice work" floats past your teammate's ears. "That pass you made under pressure in the second half was gutsy" lands in their chest and stays. God does not give generic love either. He knows every hair on your head. When you encourage, be that specific. It costs you ten extra seconds and builds something money cannot buy: trust.

Prayer

God, open my eyes to notice my teammates' effort so my words actually matter. Amen.

Practice

After your next practice, tell two teammates one specific thing they did well. Name the exact moment.

45

CORRECTION IS A GIFT, NOT AN ATTACK

"Whoever loves discipline loves knowledge, but whoever hates correction is stupid." Proverbs 12:1

Russell Wilson entered every new locker room, Wisconsin, Seattle, Denver, with the same habit. He asked coaches to be brutally honest about his weaknesses. Not because he enjoyed hearing flaws. Because he understood something most people never learn: criticism from someone who wants you to grow is one of the most valuable things you will ever receive. When coaches pointed out his footwork issues or his tendency to hold the ball too long, Wilson did not pout. He grabbed a notebook. He wrote it down. He fixed it. Your brain literally fights you here. Neuroscience research shows the amygdala processes criticism the same way it processes physical threat. Your body wants to defend, deflect, or shut down. That is biology, not weakness. But knowing this gives you power. Next time your coach corrects you and your face gets hot and your stomach drops, pause. Breathe. Remind yourself: this feeling is my brain protecting me from a danger that does not exist. The real danger is staying the same. Proverbs is shockingly blunt here. Hating correction is foolish. Loving it is the beginning of real knowledge. Champions choose the uncomfortable truth over comfortable ignorance every single time.

Prayer

Father, soften my heart when correction comes. Help me receive it as love. Amen.

Practice

Next time a coach corrects you, respond with "thank you" before anything else. Train the reflex.

46

LOOK THEM IN THE EYES

"My dear brothers and sisters, take note of this: Everyone should be quick to listen, slow to speak, and slow to become angry." James 1:19

Watch any Russell Wilson postgame interview. Watch his sideline conversations. His eyes lock onto whoever is speaking. Not glancing at the scoreboard. Not scanning the crowd. Full, undivided attention. Teammates have said publicly that Wilson made them feel like the most important person in the room simply by how he listened. In a world where everyone is half distracted, that focus became his superpower off the field.

UCLA research found that 55% of communication is nonverbal. More than half of what you "say" comes from your body, your posture, your eyes. When your coach is talking and you are staring at the ground or picking at your shoelaces, your body is screaming "I do not care" even if your brain is listening. Eye contact says: you matter, I am here, I respect you. James 1:19 is not just about patience. It is about presence. Being quick to listen means your whole body leans in. That is rare for anyone, let alone a teenager. And rare things are powerful things. Start making eye contact a habit and watch how differently people treat you.

Prayer

Jesus, teach me to be fully present when someone speaks to me. Amen.

Practice

In every conversation today, practice holding eye contact for three full seconds before responding. Notice the difference.

47

ASK BEFORE YOU ASSUME

"Plans fail for lack of counsel, but with many advisers they succeed." Proverbs 15:22

Russell Wilson became famous for a question: "Why not you?" But less known is how often Wilson asked questions of others. He called coaches before being drafted, not to pitch himself, but to ask what they needed. He approached offensive coordinators with genuine curiosity. "What do you see in my game? Where can I improve? What is the plan and how do I fit?" This was not sucking up. This was strategic humility. And it changed how coaches saw him from "undersized project" to "mature leader." Most teen athletes wait silently, hoping coaches will read their minds. Then frustration builds. "Why am I not starting? Why did the play call change?" Research published in the Journal of Sports Sciences confirms that athletes who initiate communication with coaches report 40% higher satisfaction and greater role clarity. God designed wisdom to flow through relationships, not isolation. Proverbs says plans fail without counsel. That means your growth plan needs your coach's voice in it. Walk up before or after practice. Ask one honest question. "What should I work on this week?" That single sentence separates you from 90% of your teammates. It is not weakness. It is wisdom with legs.

Prayer

Lord, give me courage to ask my coaches the questions I have been avoiding. Amen.

Practice

Before your next practice ends, ask your coach one specific question about how you can improve.

48

HANDLE IT FACE TO FACE

"If your brother or sister sins, go and point out their fault, just between the two of you." Matthew 18:15

In the 2014 Seattle Seahawks locker room, tension simmered between offense and defense after tough losses. Russell Wilson did not send group texts. He did not vent on social media. He did not gossip to one group about another. He walked across the locker room and talked to people directly, face to face, voice to voice. Teammates later said Wilson's willingness to have uncomfortable conversations privately kept the team from imploding during their most pressured season.

Here is what happens when you handle conflict over text: tone disappears. A UCLA study showed that people misinterpret the emotional tone of messages 50% of the time. Half the time. So that "I just think you should pass more" text your teammate reads? It lands as an attack, not a suggestion. Jesus gave a crystal clear blueprint in Matthew 18. Go to them. Just you two. Privately. This is terrifying for teenagers. It is terrifying for adults too. But screen courage is fake courage. Real maturity walks up, makes eye contact, and says, "Hey, can we talk about something?" That conversation, however awkward, builds respect that a hundred texts never will.

Prayer

God, give me the bravery to talk face to face when conflict comes. Amen.

Practice

If you have an unresolved issue with a teammate, commit to a private, in person conversation this week.

49

GRACE WHEN YOU ARE BENCHED

"Let your conversation be always full of grace, seasoned with salt, so that you may know how to answer everyone." Colossians 4:6

Every scout doubted Russell Wilson because of his height. But even after he proved them wrong, there were seasons where plays were not called his way, where coaches limited his role, where the game plan did not feature him. Wilson could have stormed into offices demanding more touches. Instead, he chose his words with surgical precision. He asked coaches, "What do you need from me to help us win?" Not "Why am I not getting the ball?" The difference between those two sentences is the difference between a career and a conflict. When your coach does not play you, your chest burns. You feel invisible. That is valid. But what you say next defines your trajectory. Sports psychologist Dr. Jim Taylor found that athletes who respond to reduced playing time with entitled language get fewer future opportunities, not more. Grace does not mean silence. It means speaking with respect even when your emotions are screaming. Colossians 4:6 says "seasoned with salt," meaning your words should have flavor, substance, honesty, but wrapped in respect. Walk up to your coach and say, "I want to earn more time. What do I need to work on?" That sentence is grace with salt. And it opens doors that complaining slams shut.

Prayer

Father, guard my mouth when I feel overlooked. Let my words reflect your grace. Amen.

Practice

Write down one respectful question to ask your coach about earning more playing time this week.

50

SOLUTIONS ONLY, NO COMPLAINING

"Do everything without grumbling or arguing, so that you may become blameless and pure, children of God without fault." Philippians 2:14–15

The 2015 Super Bowl interception. One yard from the championship. Russell Wilson watched the ball fly into the wrong hands and felt his dream shatter on national television. In the press conference minutes later, reporters waited for complaints. Bad play call. Wrong read. Someone else's fault. Wilson stood at the podium and said, "That is on me." No grumbling. No finger pointing. Then he went further: "We will be back. We will work harder." He replaced every possible complaint with a commitment to a solution. Complaining is a neurological habit. Neuroscience research from Stanford shows that repeated complaining rewires your brain, shrinking the hippocampus and making problem solving harder over time. Every complaint literally makes you worse at finding answers. Philippians is not asking you to be fake positive. It is protecting your brain and your witness. Next time practice is brutal, the refs are terrible, or the weather ruins your game, catch the complaint before it leaves your mouth. Replace it. "This is hard" becomes "This is making me tougher." "That call was unfair" becomes "I need to play so well that no call matters." Solutions only. That is how Wilson rebuilt after the worst moment of his career.

Prayer

Lord, transform my complaints into commitments. Make me a problem solver, not a grumbler. Amen.

Practice

Carry a small note and mark every complaint you catch yourself making today. Replace each one with a solution.

PART 7: BUILD TRUE UNITY LIKE LIONEL MESSI

51

CELEBRATE TEAMMATES' WINS

"Rejoice with those who rejoice; mourn with those who mourn." Romans 12:15

Your teammate scores the winning goal. The crowd goes crazy. But inside your chest? A gross, heavy sting. "That should have been ME." You high five them, force a smile, but it feels fake. That monster is called envy, and Stanford research proved it wrecks teams, dropping performance by 24%.

Picture the 2022 World Cup semifinal. Soccer GOAT Lionel Messi had chased this trophy his whole legendary career. When his teammate Julián Álvarez scored, Messi could have sulked on the sideline. Instead, cameras caught him sprinting full speed, grinning like a kid on Christmas morning. Pure hype for his teammate. No jealousy. No ego. Just real love. Romans 12:15 is not a suggestion. It is the formula for unbreakable teams. God's blessings never run out. There is always enough for you too. So next time your teammate goes off, do not fake clap. Actually celebrate. Go crazy for them. Because the one who cheers loudest for others never stands alone when their own moment comes. Genuine celebration rewires your brain away from scarcity.

Prayer

God, rip envy out of my heart. Fill me with real joy when my teammates win. Amen.

Practice

Text one teammate tonight something specific and awesome they did at practice today. Keep it up all week.

52

WELCOME THE NEW PLAYER

"Do not forget to show hospitality to strangers, for by so doing some people have shown hospitality to angels without knowing it." Hebrews 13:2

Remember your first day? New team. New faces. Everybody already has inside jokes. You stand at the edge of the group hoping someone, anyone, will say your name. Your stomach churns. You want to disappear. That feeling is universal, and it is brutal.

When Messi arrived at Barcelona's La Masia academy at 13, he was a tiny, quiet kid from Argentina who barely spoke to anyone. He was the outsider. Years later, as captain, Messi became known for personally greeting every single new signing, making them feel at home immediately. He remembered what loneliness tasted like. Hebrews 13:2 says strangers might be angels. That shy new kid at tryouts might become your best friend, your assist leader, your prayer partner. You will never know if you leave them standing alone. Welcoming someone is not weakness. It is leadership before you ever wear the armband.

One warm greeting can change a teammate's entire season.

Prayer

Lord, give me eyes to see the lonely and courage to walk toward them first. Amen.

Practice

At your next practice, introduce yourself to the newest or quietest player. Learn their name. Use it twice.

53

CHEMISTRY BEYOND THE FIELD

"As iron sharpens iron, so one person sharpens another." Proverbs 27:17

Some teams have all the talent but zero magic. They lose to squads half as skilled. Why? Because chemistry is not built during games. It is built in the moments nobody sees.

Messi and his Argentina teammates started a tradition years before their World Cup glory. Between matches they cooked together, played card games, stayed up laughing in hotel hallways. They called their group chat "La Scaloneta" after their coach. Those silly, ordinary moments forged something unbreakable. When they faced brutal pressure in Qatar, they did not fold because they were not just teammates. They were brothers. Proverbs 27:17 says iron sharpens iron. That sharpening happens in conversations over meals, walks home from practice, video game sessions on weekends. You cannot read someone's run on the field if you do not know their heart off it. The best teams are friends first.

Off field bonding directly predicts on field performance.

Prayer

Father, help me invest in my teammates beyond practice and games. Build us into family. Amen.

Practice

Invite two teammates to hang out this week doing something totally unrelated to your sport. Just connect.

54
SERVE WITHOUT BEING ASKED

"For even the Son of Man did not come to be served, but to serve, and to give His life as a ransom for many." Mark 10:45

Nobody posts about picking up cones. Nobody highlights the player who carries the water cooler or encourages the kid sitting on the bench with tears in their eyes. But those invisible acts? They build dynasties.

After winning the 2022 World Cup, Messi was photographed helping staff members pack equipment bags. The greatest player alive, golden trophy still warm in his hands, picking up gear. He did not think service was beneath him because he understood Mark 10:45. Jesus, the King of everything, washed dirty feet. If the Son of God serves, then serving your teammate is not weakness. It is the most powerful thing you can do. When you grab someone's water bottle without being asked, or sit next to the benchwarmer and say, "Your time is coming," you build a culture where everyone matters. That culture wins championships.

Serving teammates builds trust faster than any speech ever will.

Prayer

Jesus, make me a servant first. Let my hands build others up before they build my highlight reel. Amen.

Practice

Tomorrow at practice, do one task nobody asked you to do. Carry equipment. Encourage a reserve player. Say nothing about it.

55
RIVALRY INSIDE YOUR OWN TEAM

"Not looking to your own interests but each of you to the interests of the others." Philippians 2:4

There is someone on your team who plays your exact position. They are good. Maybe better. Every time they get picked to start, something ugly rises inside you. You want them to mess up. You catch yourself hoping they fumble, miss, stumble. Be honest. That thought has visited you.

Messi competed for playing time at Barcelona as a teenager against established superstars. He could have sabotaged or complained. Instead he trained so hard that he earned his spot, and when others played ahead of him, he cheered. Philippians 2:4 says look to the interests of others, not just your own. Here is the wild part: when you genuinely want your rival teammate to succeed, you both get sharper. Competition inside a team is healthy. Bitterness is poison. The difference is your heart. Push each other. Celebrate each other. Let the coach decide, and trust God with the outcome.

Healthy internal competition sharpens everyone when ego stays out.

Prayer

God, when jealousy whispers about my teammate, replace it with genuine respect and hunger to improve. Amen.

Practice

Compliment the teammate who competes for your position on one specific thing they do better than you. Mean it.

56
MENTOR THE YOUNGER ONES

"In everything set them an example by doing what is good." Titus 2:7

You do not need to be a senior to be a mentor. You just need to be one step ahead of someone and willing to turn around and reach back.

At Inter Miami, Messi stunned fans by spending extra time after training with young academy players, correcting their technique, encouraging their confidence. Reporters asked why the GOAT bothered with kids. His answer was simple: someone at La Masia did it for him when he was small, homesick, and scared. That is how Titus 2:7 works. You set an example not by lecturing but by doing. The 12 year old watching you handle a bad call, respond to a tough loss, or work when nobody is watching is absorbing everything. Your example shapes them before a single word leaves your mouth. Mentoring is not about being perfect. It is about being present and honest.

One older player's kindness can redirect a younger athlete's entire path.

Prayer

Lord, help me remember someone poured into me. Let me pour into the next kid coming up. Amen.

Practice

Find one younger player on your team or club this week. Show them one thing you have learned. Encourage them by name.

57
LISTEN MORE THAN YOU TALK

"Even fools are thought wise if they keep silent, and discerning if they hold their tongues." Proverbs 17:28

Loudest voice in the locker room does not equal strongest leader. Sometimes the most powerful thing you can do is close your mouth and open your ears.

Messi is famously quiet. Teammates have described him as the captain who leads with presence, not volume. In team meetings, he listens to every voice before offering his own. He absorbs. He watches. Then, when he finally speaks, every single person in the room leans in because his words carry weight. Proverbs 17:28 says silence can look like wisdom. When you actually listen to a teammate's frustration, their idea, their fear, you make them feel valued. That is more powerful than any halftime speech. Listening tells someone, "You matter. I see you." And a team full of people who feel seen will run through walls for each other.

Listening builds trust that talking never can.

Prayer

Father, slow my tongue and sharpen my ears. Help me hear what my teammates really need. Amen.

Practice

At your next team gathering, challenge yourself to ask two questions and give zero opinions. Just listen fully.

58
TRUST TEAMMATES UNDER PRESSURE

"Two are better than one, because they have a good return for their labor."
Ecclesiastes 4:9

Final minutes. Score is tied. Everything in you screams, "I have to do this myself." You grip tighter. You force it. And it falls apart because pressure plus selfishness equals disaster.

In the 2022 World Cup final against France, the most intense match in soccer history, Messi did not try to win alone. With the game on the line, he trusted his teammates with critical passes, defensive responsibilities, and penalty kicks. He could have held the ball, forced shots, played hero. Instead, he believed in the people beside him. And they delivered. Ecclesiastes 4:9 says two are better than one. Trusting your teammate in a pressure moment is scary because you lose control. But God designed teams for a reason. You were never meant to carry everything yourself. Pass the ball. Trust the preparation. Let your people shine.

Trusting teammates in clutch moments multiplies everyone's strength exponentially.

Prayer

God, when pressure makes me grip tighter, remind me I am not alone. Help me trust my team. Amen.

Practice

In your next high pressure drill, deliberately pass to a teammate instead of taking the shot yourself. Watch what happens.

59

EAT TOGETHER, BOND TOGETHER

"Every day they continued to meet together in the temple courts. They broke bread in their homes and ate together with glad and sincere hearts." Acts 2:46

There is something about sharing food that breaks down walls nothing else can. Not drills. Not team meetings. Not trust falls. Food.

After Argentina's World Cup matches, win or lose, the entire squad gathered for family style dinners. Messi sat with reserves. Coaches sat with physios. Nobody pulled rank. They passed plates, told stories, laughed until their sides hurt. Those meals became sacred ground where egos dissolved and brotherhood solidified. Acts 2:46 describes the early church doing the same thing: eating together with glad and sincere hearts. Something holy happens when you sit across from someone and share a meal. Walls come down. Grudges fade. Real conversations start. You do not need a fancy restaurant. Pizza after practice. Sandwiches at someone's house. The food is not the point. The presence is.

Shared meals create emotional bonds that survive competitive pressure.

Prayer

Lord, teach me that fellowship is fuel. Help me create moments where my team becomes family. Amen.

Practice

Organize a simple team meal this week. Even snacks after practice counts. Sit next to someone you do not know well.

PART 8: STAY CLUTCH LIKE SYDNEY MCLAUGHLIN-LEVRONE

61

SEE IT BEFORE YOU DO IT

"Now faith is confidence in what we hope for and assurance about what we do not see." Hebrews 11:1

Sydney McLaughlin-Levrone does not just run races in stadiums. She runs them in her mind first. Before every competition, she closes her eyes and visualizes the entire race. Not vaguely. She feels the rubber track under her spikes. She hears the starter's gun crack through the air. She smells the warm stadium turf. She sees each hurdle approaching. She feels her legs driving over them with perfect rhythm. By the time the real race begins, her brain has already completed it successfully. Neuroscience research from the Cleveland Clinic shows that mental visualization activates the same brain regions as physically performing the action. Your brain literally cannot tell the difference between a vividly imagined rep and a real one.   This is exactly what Hebrews 11:1 describes. Faith is being sure of what you cannot yet see. Sydney believed in a world record before she ran one. She saw it, felt it, lived it in her mind. You can do this too. Five minutes before practice, close your eyes. Use all five senses. See your best performance. Hear the sounds. Feel the ball, the water, the track. When you step into the real moment, your brain whispers, "Oh, I have been here before." That is when nerves turn into confidence.

Prayer

Lord, give me eyes of faith to see victory before it happens. I trust You. Amen.

Practice

Set a timer for five minutes tonight. Close your eyes and visualize tomorrow's practice using all five senses. Do this daily.

62

ONE WORD THAT LOCKS YOU IN

"Fixing our eyes on Jesus, the pioneer and perfecter of faith." Hebrews 12:2

Mid-race, with lactic acid screaming through her legs and the crowd roaring so loud she could feel it in her ribs, Sydney McLaughlin-Levrone does not think about her competitors. She does not think about the clock. She uses a single focus cue to snap her mind back to the present. One word. For her, it connects to her faith. It pulls her out of panic and drops her straight into purpose. Sports psychologists call these "anchor words," and research from the Journal of Applied Sport Psychology confirms they reduce anxiety and sharpen focus by giving your brain one clear job instead of a thousand spinning worries.

Hebrews 12:2 says to fix your eyes on Jesus. Not on the scoreboard. Not on the stands. Not on your opponent. One fixed point. That is how focus works. Your brain cannot chase two thoughts at full speed. So pick your word. "Smooth." "Strong." "His." Whatever anchors you. When the moment gets loud and your thoughts start spiraling, whisper that word. It is like a reset button for your brain. Sydney does not fight distractions. She replaces them. One word, one focus, one God. That is how you lock in when everything around you is chaos.

Prayer

Jesus, be my fixed point. When everything gets loud, let me hear only You. Amen.

Practice

Choose one focus word today. Write it on your wrist or shoe. Use it every time your mind wanders during practice this week.

63

SAME STEPS, AGAIN

"But everything should be done in a fitting and orderly way." 1 Corinthians 14:40

Watch Sydney McLaughlin-Levrone before any race and you will notice something fascinating. The same stretches. The same prayer posture. The same way she adjusts her blocks. The same deep breath before she settles into her stance. It never changes. Whether it is a local meet or an Olympic final, her pre-race routine is identical. This is not superstition. It is science. Research from the University of Calgary found that athletes with consistent pre-performance routines experienced significantly lower anxiety and higher confidence. A routine tells your brain, "We have done this before. We are safe. We are ready." God is a God of order. First Corinthians 14:40 reminds us that things done in a fitting and orderly way carry power. Sydney's routine is not about control. It is about surrender. Each step brings her closer to a place of peace where she can let go and let God move through her. You need your own routine. Maybe it is three deep breaths, a quick prayer, and bouncing on your toes. Maybe it is listening to a worship song and stretching in the same order. Whatever it is, lock it in and repeat it every time. When the pressure cranks up, your routine becomes your anchor. Your body relaxes because it recognizes the pattern. Chaos cannot touch a mind that is already ordered.

Prayer

God, help me build routines that bring order to my chaos and peace to my nerves. Amen.

Practice

Design a three-step pre-game routine today. Write it down. Use it before every practice and game this week without skipping.

64

BE IN YOUR CIRCLE

"Therefore do not worry about tomorrow, for tomorrow will worry about itself. Each day has enough trouble of its own." Matthew 6:34

Before the Paris Olympics, journalists kept asking Sydney McLaughlin-Levrone about defending her title, about rivals closing the gap, about the weight of expectations. She could have spiraled into worry about things completely outside her control. Instead, she stayed inside her circle. She focused on her training, her recovery, her faith, and her preparation. She could not control the weather, the lane assignments, how fast her competitors ran, or what millions of people thought. So she released all of it. Research from the American Psychological Association shows that athletes who focus only on controllable factors experience 30% less competitive anxiety.

Jesus said it plainly in Matthew 6:34. Do not worry about tomorrow. Each day has enough of its own challenges. Imagine drawing two circles on paper. The inner circle holds everything you can control: your effort, your attitude, your preparation, your response. The outer circle holds everything you cannot: refs, weather, opponents, crowd noise, results. Sydney lives in the inner circle. Most athletes who choke are mentally standing in the outer circle, stressing over things they were never meant to carry. Move back inside. Control your effort. Control your attitude. Release the rest to God. That is where clutch athletes live.

Prayer

Father, show me what is mine to carry and what is Yours. I release the rest. Amen.

Practice

Draw two circles on paper. List what you can and cannot control before your next competition. Focus only on the inner circle.

65

LOVE THE PROCESS

"Commit to the Lord whatever you do, and He will establish your plans."
Proverbs 16:3

Sydney McLaughlin-Levrone has said in multiple interviews that she does not step onto the track thinking about gold medals. She thinks about executing her race. Hitting her marks. Driving her arms. Staying in rhythm over each hurdle. The outcome, the time on the clock, the place she finishes, those are byproducts of doing the process right. When she broke the world record at the Tokyo Olympics, she did not even realize it until she looked at the scoreboard. She was that locked into each step. Research published in the Journal of Sports Sciences confirms that process-focused athletes consistently outperform outcome-focused athletes, especially under high-pressure conditions.

Proverbs 16:3 says to commit your work to God and He will establish the plans. Not your results. Your work. Your daily reps. Your effort in the film room. Your honesty in recovery. God does not ask you to guarantee a trophy. He asks you to show up and give your best. The trophy is His department. When you stop obsessing over the scoreboard and start obsessing over getting better every single day, something shifts inside you. Pressure drops. Joy increases. And weirdly, the results start taking care of themselves. Sydney did not chase world records. She chased process. The records chased her.

Prayer

Lord, I commit my daily work to You. Help me trust You with the results. Amen.

Practice

Before your next game, write down three process goals instead of outcome goals. Focus only on executing those three things.

66
BREATHE LIKE A CHAMPION

"Be still, and know that I am God." Psalm 46:10

Seconds before the gun fires, Sydney McLaughlin-Levrone takes one slow, deliberate breath. Not a panicked gulp of air. A controlled, deep breath that tells her nervous system, "We are calm. We are ready." This is not just a habit. It is biology. Box breathing, a technique used by Navy SEALs and elite athletes, involves inhaling for four counts, holding for four, exhaling for four, and holding again for four. Research from the International Journal of Psychophysiology shows this pattern activates your parasympathetic nervous system, dropping your heart rate and cortisol levels within sixty seconds. Your body physically shifts from "fight or flight" to "focused and ready."   Psalm 46:10 commands us to be still and know that He is God. Stillness is not weakness. It is the most powerful thing you can do when everything inside you is screaming to panic. Sydney chooses stillness before she chooses speed. You can too. When your hands shake before a big moment, do not fight the shaking. Breathe through it. Four counts in. Hold four. Four counts out. Hold four. Repeat three times. Your heart slows. Your mind clears. Your hands steady. You just told your brain that you are not in danger. You are in position. God meets you in the stillness, and from that stillness, you explode into action.

Prayer

God, teach me to be still even when everything feels urgent. You are my calm. Amen.

Practice

Practice box breathing tonight before bed. Four counts in, hold four, out four, hold four. Use it before your next competition.

67
PURPOSE OVER PERFECTION

"My grace is sufficient for you, for my power is made perfect in weakness." 2 Corinthians 12:9

At the 2019 World Championships, Sydney McLaughlin-Levrone finished second. Not first. Second. She clipped a hurdle. Her rhythm broke. By the world's standards, she fell short. But Sydney did not spiral into self-destruction. She did not call herself a failure. She went back to training, back to prayer, back to purpose. Because Sydney does not run for perfection. She runs for God's glory. And God's glory does not require a flawless performance. It requires a willing heart. When she later broke world records at back-to-back Olympics, those victories were built on the foundation of that "imperfect" race where she chose purpose over perfection. Second Corinthians 12:9 flips everything upside down. God's power is made perfect in weakness. Not in your highlight reel. In your weakness. That means your worst game, your messiest performance, your most embarrassing moment can be the exact place where God shows up the strongest. Perfectionism tells you that anything less than flawless is worthless. That is a lie. Purpose says, "I will give my absolute best and trust God with the gaps." Sydney gave herself permission to be imperfect and that freedom is exactly what unlocked her greatest performances. Stop trying to be perfect. Start trying to be faithful

Prayer

Lord, free me from perfectionism. Let my purpose be bigger than my performance. Amen.

Practice

After your next competition, write down one thing you did well and one thing to improve. Skip all self-criticism. Just grow.

PART 9: MASTER DAILY DISCIPLINE LIKE KOBE BRYANT

68

PLAN YOUR TIME LIKE A PRO

"Be very careful, then, how you live, not as unwise but as wise, making the most of every opportunity." Ephesians 5:15-16

Kobe Bryant did not just wake up at 4 AM and wing it. Every single hour of his day had a purpose. His morning was shooting drills. Mid-morning was film study. Afternoon was team practice. Evening was recovery. He mapped his days so tightly that people called him obsessive, but Kobe called it stewardship. He believed God gave him 24 hours just like everyone else, and wasting even one was disrespectful to that gift. "You can't get time back," he once told a group of young players. "Money comes back. Time never does."   Maybe your life feels chaotic. School, practice, homework, family stuff, all crashing into each other. You forget assignments. You show up late. You feel overwhelmed and then just scroll your phone because everything feels like too much. That is not a laziness problem. That is a planning problem. Neuroscience confirms our brains perform better when tasks are externalized onto paper rather than juggled mentally. Kobe treated his schedule like his playbook. You do not need a fancy app. Grab a simple weekly planner or even a sheet of paper. Write tomorrow's top three priorities tonight before bed. When you plan your time, you honor what God gave you.

Prayer

Lord, teach me to value every hour You give me and spend them wisely. Amen.

Practice

Tonight, write tomorrow's schedule on paper: school, practice, study, rest. Follow it for five days straight.

69

OWN YOUR GEAR, OWN YOUR LIFE

"Whoever can be trusted with very little can also be trusted with much." Luke 16:10

Before Kobe became the player who outworked everyone, he was a teenager whose father, Joe "Jellybean" Bryant, taught him a simple rule: pack your own bag. Every game. Every practice. No exceptions. Nobody else checks your shoes, your water, your gear. That is your responsibility. Kobe carried this habit his entire career. He personally inspected his shoes before every game, checked his jersey, organized his locker. Small? Sure. But Kobe understood something powerful: the way you handle small things reveals how you will handle big things. God was watching his faithfulness in the details long before the championships arrived.   You probably let your mom or dad pack your sports bag sometimes. Maybe you have shown up to practice missing a shin guard or forgotten your water bottle. It feels minor, but here is what is really happening: you are training your brain to depend on someone else for things you can control. Research on adolescent autonomy shows that teens who manage their own daily logistics develop stronger executive function and self-confidence. Packing your bag is not about a bag. It is about telling yourself, "I own my preparation. I am responsible for me." That tiny act of faithfulness builds the muscle for much bigger moments.

Prayer

God, help me be faithful in small things so You can trust me with greater ones. Amen.

Practice

Pack your practice bag completely by yourself tonight. Check every item off a list. Do it every day this week.

70
GRADES ARE YOUR INSURANCE POLICY

"The heart of the discerning acquires knowledge, for the ears of the wise seek it out." Proverbs 18:15

Kobe Bryant graduated from Lower Merion High School with SAT scores high enough to attend any top university in America. He chose the NBA draft instead, but he never treated school as optional. His parents made academics non-negotiable, and Kobe later credited that discipline for his ability to study game film like a scholar. He learned Italian fluently as a child living in Italy, spoke Spanish, and consumed books on psychology and business throughout his life. His mind was as trained as his body. Kobe often said that basketball careers end, but a sharp mind lasts forever.   Maybe you think grades do not matter because you are going to go pro. Here is the truth that stings: fewer than 2% of high school athletes earn college scholarships. Fewer than 0.01% go professional. That is not meant to crush your dream. Chase it with everything. But academics are your backup plan, your insurance policy, your proof that you are disciplined in every arena. Studies show that student athletes with higher GPAs actually perform better in competition because academic discipline strengthens focus and mental endurance. God gave you a brain and a body. Honoring only one while ignoring the other is half-obedience.

Prayer

Lord, give me hunger for knowledge and discipline to prioritize my education always. Amen.

Practice

Set a daily 30-minute study block this week. No phone. No music. Just focused learning before or after practice.

71

DREAM MONTHLY, WEEKLY, TODAY

"The plans of the diligent lead to profit as surely as haste leads to poverty."
Proverbs 21:5

Kobe Bryant did not just say, "I want to win championships." He reverse-engineered it. He started with the dream: become the greatest basketball player ever. Then he broke it into seasons. Then months. Then weeks. Then each day's specific workout. His trainer Tim Grover revealed that Kobe would set targets like "improve left-hand finishing by 15% this month" and then design daily drills to hit that exact number. Nothing was vague. Nothing was "I'll just try harder." Every dream had a blueprint, and every blueprint had a deadline. Kobe believed God honored specific plans backed by relentless action.

You probably have big dreams. Maybe you want to make varsity, earn a scholarship, or represent your country. But if someone asked you, "What are you doing this Wednesday at 3 PM to get closer to that dream?" could you answer? Most teens cannot. That is the gap between dreamers and achievers. Psychological research on goal specificity shows that people who write concrete weekly and daily goals are 42% more likely to achieve them. Your dream is the mountain. Your monthly goal is the trail. Your weekly goal is the next mile marker. Now is your very next step.

Prayer

Father, help me turn my big dreams into small, faithful daily steps of obedience. Amen.

Practice

Write one big dream, one monthly goal, one weekly target, and one thing to do today. Start now.

72
TRACK PROGRESS

"Write down the revelation and make it plain on tablets so that a herald may run with it." Habakkuk 2:2

Kobe Bryant kept detailed notebooks throughout his career. Not digital notes. Handwritten pages filled with observations from games, weaknesses he noticed in his own play, and specific improvements he wanted to make. After rewatching film, he would write down exactly what he saw and what he planned to change. His notebooks became his personal coaching manual. When asked why he did not just use technology, Kobe explained that writing by hand forced his brain to process information more deeply. He treated those notebooks like sacred documents, a written conversation between his current self and his future self, guided by the purpose God placed in him.

You have probably tried tracking things on your phone and quit after three days. Notifications pop up, you start scrolling, and suddenly your "progress tracker" becomes a distraction machine. Neuroscience backs Kobe's instinct: handwriting activates deeper memory encoding than typing. A simple notebook where you log three things daily, what you trained, what you learned, what you will improve, becomes a powerful mirror. Over weeks, you will actually see your growth on paper. God told Habakkuk to write the vision down for a reason. What is written becomes real. What stays in your head stays fuzzy. Recommended Reading: The Mamba Mentality: How I Play by Kobe Bryant

---

Prayer

Lord, help me write down my growth so I can see Your faithfulness over time. Amen.

Practice

Buy a small notebook today. Each night, write what you trained, learned, and will improve tomorrow.

73

SOLVE IT BEFORE YOU ASK

"For the Lord gives wisdom; from His mouth come knowledge and understanding." Proverbs 2:6

When Kobe was a young player, he would watch film of opponents for hours before asking coaches for their scouting reports. He wanted to figure it out himself first. He studied Michael Jordan's footwork frame by frame, tried to decode it on his own, and only then asked coaches to fill in the gaps. This habit made him one of the most basketball-intelligent players in history. Kobe believed that God gave him a brain capable of solving problems, and relying on others before even attempting to think was laziness disguised as humility. He wanted his questions to come from effort, not from avoidance. When something gets hard, what is your first instinct? If it is immediately asking a parent, coach, or friend to fix it, you are training your brain to be dependent. This does not mean you should never ask for help. But try first. Struggle with it for ten minutes. Research from educational psychology shows that productive struggle, the effort before the answer, is where real learning happens. Your brain literally builds stronger neural pathways when it wrestles with a problem before receiving the solution. God promises wisdom to those who seek it. Seeking means searching, not just waiting for someone to hand it to you.

Prayer

God, give me courage to think hard and seek wisdom before I ask for easy answers. Amen.

Practice

Next time you face a problem, spend ten full minutes trying to solve it yourself before asking anyone.

74

JOURNAL THREE DAILY WINS

"Praise the Lord, my soul, and forget not all His benefits." Psalm 103:2

Even during seasons when Kobe's body was breaking down from injuries and his team was losing, he maintained a habit of recognizing what went right each day. He would identify specific plays where his technique improved, moments where his conditioning held up, or times his leadership made a difference. Kobe refused to let bad days erase small victories. He once told a young player, "You had a terrible game, but your defense in the third quarter was elite. Build on that." His Catholic faith taught him gratitude was not optional. Thanking God for daily blessings, even small ones, kept his perspective sharp and his spirit resilient.   Your brain has a negativity bias. Science confirms it: humans remember negative experiences more vividly than positive ones. After a bad practice, you probably replay every mistake on a loop and forget the three things you actually did well. This is not just discouraging. It physically rewires your brain toward hopelessness over time. Positive psychology research shows that writing three wins daily, no matter how small, retrains your brain to notice progress instead of only failure. "I made that one good pass." "I did not quit during conditioning." "I encouraged a teammate." These matter. God says to forget not His benefits. Writing them down makes forgetting impossible.

Prayer

Lord, open my eyes to three good things today and help me thank You for each one. Amen.

Practice

Every night this week, write three wins from the day in your notebook. They can be tiny. Just write them.

75
BUILD A ROUTINE THAT STICKS

"In the morning, Lord, you hear my voice; in the morning I lay my requests before you and wait expectantly." Psalm 5:3

Kobe's mornings were legendary. While the world slept, he was already in the gym at 4 AM. But his routine was not just physical. Before the sweat and the shooting drills, Kobe attended early morning Mass or spent time in private prayer. He built a morning sequence that fed his spirit, then his mind, then his body, in that order. He did not check his phone first. He did not scroll through highlights or news. He started with God, moved to mental preparation, then attacked his physical training. This order was intentional. Kobe believed that a morning won before the world wakes up creates a day that cannot be stolen from you. You probably wake up, grab your phone, scroll for twenty minutes, and then rush through everything else. Research on morning routines shows that the first 30 minutes of your day set your brain's emotional tone for the next 12 hours. Starting with screens floods your mind with other people's agendas. Starting with prayer, a quick stretch, and a glance at your goals floods your mind with purpose. You do not need to wake up at 4 AM. But you do need a sequence that is yours. Even 15 minutes of intentional morning structure changes everything. God hears your voice in the morning. Make sure He is the first one who gets it.

Prayer

God, meet me every morning before the noise begins. Help me start each day with You. Amen.

Practice

Set your alarm 15 minutes earlier tomorrow. Pray, stretch, and review your goals before touching your phone.

76

SHOW UP WHEN YOU DO NOT FEEL IT

"I discipline my body and keep it under control, lest after preaching to others I myself should be disqualified." 1 Corinthians 9:27

There is a famous story about Kobe showing up to practice with the flu so severe that teammates told him to go home. He refused. He did not have a great practice. His shot was off, his energy was low, and he looked exhausted. But he still went through every drill. Afterward, a reporter asked why he came in sick. Kobe said, "Because the days I don't feel like showing up are the most important days to show up. That's when discipline gets built." His faith reinforced this conviction. Kobe saw his talent as God-given and believed that discipline was the way he proved he was grateful for it.   This is the foundation where most teens quit. Motivation gets you to start. Discipline gets you to stay. You will have mornings where your bed feels like a magnet. Practices where your legs feel like concrete. Days where nothing inside you wants to try. Behavioral science confirms that consistency on low-motivation days is the single strongest predictor of long-term success in any field. Not talent. Not resources. Consistency. Paul wrote about disciplining his body because he understood that feelings are terrible leaders. They change hourly. Your commitment should not. The version of you that shows up when you do not feel like it is the version that becomes unstoppable.

Prayer

Lord, give me strength to show up faithfully even when everything in me wants to quit. Amen.

Practice

Next time you want to skip practice or a workout, go anyway. Just show up. That one choice changes everything.

PART 10: NEVER STOP IMPROVING LIKE USAIN BOLT

77

WATCH FILM LIKE A STUDENT

"The discerning heart seeks knowledge, but the mouth of a fool feeds on folly." Proverbs 15:14

The 2008 Beijing Olympics. Usain Bolt crossed the 100m finish line so far ahead he slowed down to celebrate, arms spread wide, chest out, grinning at the sky. The world gasped. "Pure talent," they said. "Born to run." But back in Kingston, Jamaica, Bolt's coach Glen Mills had spent hundreds of hours breaking down film frame by frame with his sprinter. They studied Bolt's own race footage obsessively. Every arm angle. Every stride length. Every millisecond lost in the drive phase. Bolt, a devout Christian, understood that God gave him speed but knowledge sharpened it.

Researcher Anders Ericsson found that elite performers review their own performance footage far more than average ones. They don't just watch, they hunt for patterns. You can do this too. Fifteen minutes a week. Watch yourself at practice on someone's phone. Then watch a pro in your sport. Compare. Where do your shoulders sit? Where are your eyes? You will spot things your feelings never told you. Discernment is not just a Bible word. It is a competitive advantage.

Prayer

Lord, give me eyes that see what I am missing so I can grow. Amen.

Practice

Record one drill at practice this week. Watch it twice. Write down two things you notice and one thing a pro does differently.

78
FUNDAMENTALS BEFORE FLASH

"They are like a man building a house, who dug down deep and laid the foundation on rock." Luke 6:48

Everyone remembers Bolt's legendary celebration, the "Lightning Bolt" pose. Nobody remembers the years he spent mastering the most boring part of sprinting: his start. Bolt was actually slow out of the blocks for most of his career. At 6'5", unfolding his long frame from a crouched position was awkward and clunky. Instead of chasing flashy top speed, Coach Mills made him drill starts over and over. Hundreds of block sessions. Tiny, invisible adjustments. Bolt later said, "I prayed every night. I trained every morning. The talent was God's gift. The work was my response."

Jesus told the parable of two builders for a reason. The flashy house looked great until the storm hit. You want the crossover that breaks ankles? Master the basic dribble first. You want the diving header? Perfect the simple pass. Ericsson's research proves that skipping fundamentals creates a ceiling you will always hit. The kid who drills basics with patience will eventually fly past the kid who rushed to look cool. Dig deep. Lay your foundation on rock. The fancy stuff will come, and when it does, it will actually hold.

Prayer

Father, give me patience to love the basics and trust the process You designed. Amen.

Practice

Pick the most basic skill in your sport. Spend ten minutes this week drilling only that, with zero shortcuts, zero rushing.

79
FIFTEEN INVISIBLE MINUTES

"And whatever you do, in word or deed, do everything in the name of the Lord Jesus." Colossians 3:17

Nine Olympic gold medals. The world saw Usain Bolt dance on the track like running was a party. What the world never saw was the quiet gym at 5 AM in Jamaica. No cameras. No fans. No music. Just Bolt and a set of resistance bands, working on hip mobility drills so boring they would put you to sleep. Fifteen minutes of focused, invisible work every single day. Not for Instagram. Not for his coach's approval. For the craft itself, offered to God like a quiet prayer.

Here is a truth that will change everything for you: fifteen minutes of alone, focused, intentional practice every day beats two hours of distracted team practice. Ericsson called it deliberate practice, training at the edge of your ability with full concentration. Most athletes train on autopilot, repeating what already feels comfortable. That is not growth. That is just movement. Your invisible fifteen minutes are sacred. Lock in. No phone. No music. Just you and one specific skill. Nobody will clap. Nobody will post about it. But God sees it, and your future self will thank you.

Prayer

Jesus, help me honor You in the work nobody sees. Make my secret effort matter. Amen.

Practice

Set a daily alarm. Fifteen minutes. One skill. Alone. Fully focused. Start today and do not skip tomorrow.

80

SLOW DOWN TO SPEED UP

"For it is precept upon precept, precept upon precept, line upon line, line upon line, here a little, there a little." Isaiah 28:10

Young Usain Bolt wanted to blast out of every practice rep at full speed. His coach Glen Mills had a different idea. He made Bolt run at reduced speed, sometimes 50%, sometimes even slower, focusing entirely on the mechanics of each phase. Bolt hated it. It felt pointless. But Mills understood something science later confirmed: motor learning research shows that practicing a movement slowly allows your brain to encode the correct pattern deeply before adding speed. Bolt's nine gold medals were built in slow motion first.

You feel this pressure too. Everyone around you is going full speed, and slowing down feels like falling behind. But think about Isaiah 28:10. God teaches "here a little, there a little." He is not in a rush, and your development should not be either. Try this: take your weakest skill and practice it at 25% speed. Feel every tiny movement. Where is your weight? Where are your hands? Once your body owns that pattern, speed will come naturally. Rushing creates sloppy habits. Patience creates mastery. Slow is smooth, and smooth eventually becomes unstoppable.

Prayer

God, teach me patience in my progress. Help me trust slow and steady growth. Amen.

Practice

Choose one skill. Practice it at quarter speed for five minutes. Only add speed once the slow version feels automatic.

81

ASK BETTER QUESTIONS

"Instruct the wise and they will be wiser still; teach the righteous and they will add to their learning." Proverbs 9:9

After every race, Usain Bolt did not walk up to his coach and say, "How was that?" He asked specific questions. "Was my third step too wide?" "Did I lose my lean at 60 meters?" "Where exactly did I tighten up?" Those targeted questions gave Coach Mills something real to work with. Bolt created a feedback loop so tight that every single race, even the ones he won easily, became a learning experience. This was not arrogance. It was hunger disguised as humility.

Most young athletes either avoid feedback entirely or ask vague questions like "Was I good?" That gives coaches nothing to work with and gives you nothing to fix. Ericsson's research shows that a tight feedback loop, where you perform, get specific input, adjust, and repeat, is the single fastest path to improvement. Proverbs says the wise get wiser because they keep seeking knowledge. After your next practice, ask your coach one sharp question: "What is one specific thing I can fix by Thursday?" Then actually fix it. The athletes who grow fastest are not the most talented. They are the most coachable.

Prayer

Lord, make me brave enough to ask hard questions and humble enough to listen. Amen.

Practice

After your next practice, ask your coach one specific question about one specific skill. Write down the answer and act on it.

82

INTENSITY OVER HOURS

"Whatever you do, work at it with all your heart, as working for the Lord, not for human masters." Colossians 3:23

There is a myth that Usain Bolt trained longer than everyone else. He did not. Bolt's training sessions were surprisingly short compared to many elite athletes. But every second was on fire. His coach designed sessions built around maximum intensity in focused bursts. Bolt gave 100% mental engagement to every rep, every drill, every sprint. No joking around during sets. No half speed warm up laps treated as real work. When it was time to train, he was completely locked in. When it was done, he rested completely.

You have probably had those two hour practices where you were physically present but mentally somewhere else. Your body moved but your brain checked out. That is junk volume. It fills time but builds nothing. Science confirms that 30 minutes of fully engaged, intentional training outperforms two hours of going through the motions. Colossians 3:23 does not say "do a lot." It says "work with all your heart." God cares about the quality of your effort, not just the quantity. Next practice, pretend every single rep is being recorded for your highlight reel. That shift in intensity changes everything.

Prayer

Father, help me bring my whole heart to every rep, not just my body. Amen.

Practice

At your next practice, pick one 20 minute block. Go 100% focused intensity. No coasting. See how different it feels.

83

THE MIRROR NEVER LIES

"For now we see only a reflection as in a mirror; then we shall see face to face." 1 Corinthians 13:12

In the training facility in Jamaica, Bolt would sometimes practice starts in front of a mirror. It sounds simple, almost silly. But the mirror revealed truths his feelings hid. He thought his arms were driving straight. The mirror showed a slight twist. He thought his head was neutral. The mirror showed it tilting left. These tiny form corrections, invisible in real time, became visible in the reflection. Bolt did not rely on how things felt. He relied on what was actually true.

Paul wrote about mirrors in 1 Corinthians because he understood that our self perception is imperfect. We think we know how we look, how we move, how we act. But we only see a dim reflection. Mirror training is one of the cheapest, most powerful tools in any athlete's toolbox. Stand in front of a mirror and perform your basic movements. Shoot your free throw form. Shadow your swim stroke. Practice your stance. You will be shocked at what you discover. The mirror is honest when your brain is not. Use it. Let truth correct you now so greatness can find you later.

Prayer

God, show me what I cannot see about myself. Give me courage to correct it. Amen.

Practice

Find a mirror. Spend five minutes practicing your sport's basic movement in front of it. Fix one thing you notice.

84

KNOW YOUR SPORT'S RULES

"Similarly, anyone who competes as an athlete does not receive the victor's crown except by competing according to the rules." 2 Timothy 2:5

At the 2011 World Championships in Daegu, Bolt experienced one of his most painful moments. He false started in the 100m final and was immediately disqualified. Gone. No race. No chance. The rule was clear: one false start and you are out. Bolt knew the rule but let his eagerness override his discipline. He later said that moment taught him to respect the boundaries of his sport as much as the speed. Rules were not obstacles. They were the structure that made the victory meaningful.

Here is a reality most young athletes ignore: you can be the most talented person on the field and still lose because you did not know a rule. Offsides. Lane violations. Equipment regulations. Time limits. These are not boring details. They are the boundaries God built into competition. Paul told Timothy that the crown only goes to athletes who compete according to the rules. Read your sport's rulebook. Seriously. Most of your competitors never will. Knowing the rules gives you an edge that talent alone cannot provide. Respect the structure, and the structure will protect your victories.

Prayer

Lord, help me respect the rules of my sport and compete with full integrity. Amen.

Practice

Find your sport's official rulebook online. Read one section this week. Learn one rule you did not fully understand before.

85

MAP YOUR SKILL PROGRESSION

"The path of the righteous is like the morning sun, shining ever brighter till the full light of day." Proverbs 4:18

Bolt's career was not a sudden explosion. It was a mapped journey. At 15, he was a 200m runner with raw talent and sloppy mechanics. By 17, he was a junior world champion still full of technical flaws. By 21, he was breaking world records. By 25, he was untouchable. Each phase built on the last. His coaches created a clear skill progression: first fix the start, then refine the drive phase, then optimize top end speed, then master race strategy. Nothing was random. Every season had a purpose.

You need a map too. Not a vague goal like "get better." A real progression. What is the most basic version of your next skill? What does the intermediate version look like? What does mastery look like? Write it down. Proverbs 4:18 says your path shines brighter and brighter. That means growth is supposed to be gradual and visible, like a sunrise. You will not wake up tomorrow as a completely different athlete. But if you follow a clear map, you will look back in six months and barely recognize the player you used to be. That slow glow is God's design.

Prayer

Father, light my path one step at a time. Help me trust Your timeline for my growth. Amen.

Practice

Write down one skill you want to master. Break it into three levels: beginner, intermediate, and advanced. Start at beginner this week.

PART 11: REST TO RESTORE LIKE SIMONE BILES

86

SLEEP LIKE A CHAMPION

"In vain you rise early and stay up late, toiling for food to eat, for He grants sleep to those He loves." Psalm 127:2

Tokyo 2021. Every camera, every headline, every expectation pointed at Simone Biles, the greatest gymnast alive. Then she did the unthinkable. She withdrew. Not from injury. From exhaustion, mental fog, a body screaming for rest. Critics went wild. But Simone stood firm: "I had to focus on my mental health. I knew God had a bigger plan." Three years later at the 2024 Paris Olympics, she returned rested, recharged, and absolutely dominant, winning gold again.

Stanford researchers found that athletes sleeping under eight hours had 1.7 times more injuries. Sleep is when your muscles actually rebuild, when your brain files away everything you learned at practice. You think grinding late makes you tougher? God literally designed sleep as a gift for the people He loves. Simone lost nothing by resting. She gained everything. You stay up until midnight rewatching highlights, then drag yourself to morning practice half asleep, wondering why your reaction time is garbage. Nine hours of sleep is not lazy. It is your secret weapon. The pillow is part of the training plan.

Prayer

Lord, help me honor my body with real sleep. You made rest a gift. I receive it. Amen.

Practice

Set a bedtime alarm tonight for nine hours before your wake up time. Hit it every night this week.

87

SCREENS OFF, PEACE ON

"In peace I will lie down and sleep, for you alone, Lord, make me dwell in safety." Psalm 4:8

Before Simone Biles returned for the 2024 Paris Games, she overhauled her entire recovery routine. One major shift? Protecting her nights. She talked openly about limiting social media, stepping away from the noise, guarding her peace. In Tokyo, the digital pressure had been relentless. Millions of opinions flooding her phone every second. By Paris, she had learned that what she consumed before sleep shaped how she performed the next day.

Harvard Medical School confirmed that blue light from screens suppresses melatonin by 50%, the exact hormone your body needs to fall into deep, restorative sleep. Your brain cannot switch from scrolling TikTok to resting peacefully. It stays wired, alert, buzzing. You lie there staring at the ceiling wondering why you cannot sleep. That is not insomnia. That is a screen problem. God promises peace when you lie down, but you have to create the conditions for it. One hour before bed, put the phone in another room. Read scripture. Stretch. Breathe. Let your mind go quiet. The notifications will still be there tomorrow. Your recovery cannot wait.

Prayer

God, give me discipline to put screens down and let Your peace fill my mind tonight. Amen.

Practice

Tonight, set your phone on a charger in another room one full hour before bed. Journal instead.

88

BUILD YOUR REST CAVE

"Come with me by yourselves to a quiet place and get some rest." Mark 6:31

Even Jesus told His disciples to pull away. They had been healing people, teaching crowds, pouring themselves out nonstop. He did not say "push harder." He said come rest. Simone Biles understood this instinct. After Tokyo, she created boundaries around her personal space, her recovery environment, the places where she could truly decompress. She was not running from gymnastics. She was running toward restoration.

Sleep scientists at the National Sleep Foundation found that a dark, cool room between 65 and 68 degrees increases deep sleep stages by up to 30%. Deep sleep is where human growth hormone floods your muscles, repairing every micro tear from training. Light leaking through curtains, a warm stuffy room, background TV noise, all of it robs you. Your bedroom should feel like a cave. Dark. Cool. Quiet. You would never train in a chaotic gym with broken equipment. So why would you try to recover in a loud, bright, overheated room? Jesus intentionally led His people to quiet places. Build yours. Blackout curtains, a fan, and zero distractions. Your body will thank you every single morning.

Prayer

Jesus, lead me to quiet places where my body and soul can truly recover and be refreshed. Amen.

Practice

Tonight, make your room darker and cooler. Remove one light source and crack a window or turn on a fan.

89

RECOVERY DAYS ARE TRAINING DAYS

"Six days do your work, but on the seventh day do not work, so that your ox and your donkey may rest, and so that the slave born in your household and the foreigner living among you may be refreshed." Exodus 23:12

When Simone Biles stepped away from competition in Tokyo, many people assumed she was doing nothing. The truth? She was actively recovering. Light movement, therapy, walking, breathing exercises. She was not sitting on a couch feeling sorry for herself. She was restoring her body with intention. Active recovery is not the same as being lazy. It is strategic rebuilding.

The British Journal of Sports Medicine found that active recovery, like light swimming, walking, or yoga, reduces next day muscle soreness by 25% compared to complete inactivity. God did not invent the Sabbath because He was tired. He modeled it because He knew we would need permission to stop. You feel guilty on rest days. You think your competitors are out there getting ahead. But your muscles do not grow during training. They grow during recovery. Overtraining tears you down without giving your body the chance to rebuild. Take your off day seriously. Walk. Stretch. Play with your dog. Move gently. Let God do the rebuilding work He designed your body to do.

Prayer

Father, teach me that rest is obedience, not weakness. Help me recover with the same discipline I train. Amen.

Practice

On your next off day, do 20 minutes of light walking or easy stretching instead of extra training.

90
ROLL OUT THE TENSION

"Dear friend, I pray that you may enjoy good health and that all may go well with you, even as your soul is getting along well." 3 John 1:2

Simone Biles has talked openly about how much time she spends on body maintenance, not just gymnastics skills. Foam rolling, stretching, physical therapy. The work nobody films. The unglamorous hours that keep her muscles healthy and her joints moving freely. At the highest level, the athletes who last are not just the most talented. They are the ones who take care of their bodies daily.

Self-myofascial release, basically foam rolling, breaks up tight fascia and increases blood flow to sore muscles. Research in the Journal of Athletic Training showed it improves range of motion by 10% and reduces soreness significantly after hard sessions. Your body stores tension everywhere, tight calves, locked up hips, knotted shoulders. That tightness slows you down and sets you up for injury. God cares about your physical health just as much as your spiritual health. That is the whole message of 3 John 1:2. Spend ten minutes rolling out after every practice. It hurts in the moment, but it is the kind of pain that heals. Your future self will be grateful you started now.

Prayer

God, help me steward my body well. Remind me that caring for it honors You every day. Amen.

Practice

Get a foam roller or tennis ball. Spend 10 minutes after your next practice rolling out your tightest muscles.

91

SEE BURNOUT BEFORE IT SEES YOU

"He makes me lie down in green pastures, He leads me beside quiet waters, He refreshes my soul." Psalm 23:2-3

In the months before Tokyo 2021, Simone Biles noticed the signs. Practice felt heavy. Joy disappeared. Her body ached in ways that did not match her training load. She dreaded the gym, the place she had loved since childhood. Something deep inside was breaking. Burnout did not hit her overnight. It crept in slowly, like fog rolling across a field, until she could barely see the passion that once drove her.

The American Academy of Pediatrics reports youth sport burnout has increased 60% in 15 years. Warning signs include dreading practice, constant fatigue even after rest, frequent illness, declining performance, irritability, and loss of motivation. If three or more of those describe you right now, pay attention. God does not drag you through exhaustion. He makes you lie down. He leads you to quiet waters. He refreshes. Burnout is not a character flaw. It is your body and soul begging for what God already prescribed. Talk to a coach, parent, or mentor. Be honest. Simone's honesty in Tokyo saved her career and her life. Yours might too.

Prayer

Lord, give me the courage to be honest when I am burning out. Lead me to Your rest. Amen.

Practice

Check yourself against the burnout signs listed above. If three or more fit, talk to a trusted adult today.

92
A LIFE OUTSIDE YOUR SPORT

"I know that there is nothing better for people than to be happy and to do good while they live. That each of them may eat and drink and find satisfaction in all their toil; this is the gift of God." Ecclesiastes 3:12-13

After stepping back in Tokyo, Simone Biles did not just sit in a dark room replaying vault routines. She cooked. She spent time with family. She enjoyed life outside the gym. She rediscovered that she was a whole person, not just a gymnast. And when she returned to competition in 2024, that fullness made her better, not worse. She was lighter. Freer. More joyful on the floor than she had been in years.

Psychologists call this "identity diversification," and research from the University of Washington shows athletes with hobbies outside their sport report 40% less anxiety and significantly higher long term motivation. When your entire identity is your sport, every bad game feels like the end of the world. But when you also paint, play guitar, cook, build things, or read, a bad game is just a bad game. God gave you gifts beyond athletics. Explore them. They do not distract from your sport. They fuel it. The most dangerous athlete is not the obsessed one. It is the whole one.

Prayer

God, remind me I am more than my sport. Help me find joy in all the gifts You gave me. Amen.

Practice

Pick one hobby unrelated to your sport this week. Spend 30 minutes doing it with zero guilt.

93

OFF-SEASON IS ON-PURPOSE

"By the seventh day God had finished the work He had been doing; so on the seventh day He rested from all His work." Genesis 2:2

Simone Biles took three full years between Tokyo and Paris. Three years. The greatest gymnast in history did not rush back. She let her body heal. She let her mind reset. She trusted God's timing over the world's timeline. And when she returned, she was not rusty. She was radiant. She did not just compete in Paris. She dominated. Four medals. More history. Proof that planned rest produces peak performance.

God Himself rested after creation. Not because He was exhausted. Because rest completes the cycle. Your off-season is not wasted time. It is the season where your body adapts, your injuries heal, and your motivation regenerates. A study in the British Journal of Sports Medicine found that young athletes who train year round without an off-season are 70% more likely to suffer overuse injuries. Plan your rest like you plan your workouts. Schedule lighter weeks. Take a real off-season. Trust that stepping back is not falling behind. It is loading the spring. When your season comes, you will explode forward with everything you stored during the quiet months. Rest is not the opposite of training. Rest is training's best friend.

Prayer

Father, teach me to trust Your rhythm of work and rest. My off-season belongs to You. Amen.

Practice

With a parent or coach, map out your next off-season. Include rest weeks, light activity, and zero guilt days.

PART 12: FUEL YOUR BODY LIKE ALLYSON FELIX

94
HYDRATION MATH THAT WORKS

"Whoever drinks the water I give them will never thirst. Indeed, the water I give them will become in them a spring of water welling up to eternal life."
John 4:14

The stadium lights in Tokyo felt like standing under a magnifying glass. Track legend Allyson Felix, the most decorated American Olympic track athlete ever, stood in the call room before her 400-meter heat, sipping water like clockwork. Not chugging. Sipping. She had a formula burned into her routine: half her body weight in pounds, converted to ounces of water, spread across the entire day. At 125 pounds, that meant roughly 63 ounces daily, more on race days. She never winged it.

You know that feeling when cramps lock your calves mid-game and you collapse like your legs betrayed you? Studies show even 2% dehydration drops your reaction time and focus dramatically. Most teens drink water only when they are already thirsty, but thirst means you are already behind. Allyson understood her body was on loan from God. She honored it with something as simple as consistent water. Jesus offered living water that satisfies the soul forever. But your physical water intake? That is your job. Start the math today. Half your weight in ounces. Carry a bottle everywhere. Your legs will thank you Friday night.

Prayer

Lord, remind me that caring for this body honors You. Help me drink up daily. Amen.

Practice

Calculate your number right now. Half your body weight in ounces. Fill a bottle and track it tomorrow.

95
COMPLEX CARBS, REAL ENERGY

"But those who hope in the Lord will renew their strength. They will soar on wings like eagles; they will run and not grow weary, they will walk and not be faint." Isaiah 40:31

Allyson Felix never feared carbs. While social media screamed "carbs are the enemy," she loaded her plates with oatmeal, brown rice, sweet potatoes, and whole grain bread. These complex carbohydrates burned slow and steady, releasing energy across hours instead of spiking and crashing like candy or white bread. Across five Olympic Games and eleven medals, she treated food as fuel, not entertainment. She once said she wanted to return her body to God "well-used, not abused." Here is what happens when you eat sugary cereal before a Saturday morning game: you feel electric for twenty minutes, then your blood sugar crashes and your legs turn into wet noodles. Sound familiar? Complex carbs are like putting premium logs on a fire instead of crumpled newspaper. They keep you burning strong through the fourth quarter, the final set, the last lap. God promises renewed strength to those who hope in Him. But He also gave you the wisdom to choose the right fuel. Swap the energy drink for oatmeal with banana tonight. Feel the difference by tomorrow's practice. That is not boring adult advice. That is a cheat code.

Prayer

God, give me wisdom to fuel my body with what actually works, not just what tastes easy. Amen.

Practice

Replace one sugary pre-practice snack this week with oatmeal, sweet potato, or brown rice. Notice your energy.

96
PROTEIN TIMING MATTERS

"Take wheat and barley, beans and lentils, millet and spelt; put them in a storage jar and use them to make bread for yourself." Ezekiel 4:9

After a brutal training session in Los Angeles, Allyson Felix would not just collapse on the couch. Within thirty minutes of finishing, she ate protein. Grilled chicken, Greek yogurt, eggs, a protein smoothie. Every single time. She knew that her muscles were torn and screaming during workouts, and protein within that golden thirty-minute window helped rebuild them stronger than before. That discipline carried her through nearly two decades of elite sprinting while others burned out in five years.

Your muscles do not grow during practice. They grow after, when you rest and feed them. The Journal of the International Society of Sports Nutrition confirms that post-workout protein significantly improves recovery and reduces soreness. Most teens finish practice, grab chips, scroll their phones, and wonder why they feel wrecked the next day. God literally listed proteins in Ezekiel: beans, lentils, grains. He designed your body to rebuild with the right materials. You just have to deliver them on time. Keep a banana and a small bag of nuts in your gym bag. Or mix a simple shake. Thirty minutes. That is your window. Do not miss it.

Prayer

Father, help me treat recovery as seriously as training. My body rebuilds when I cooperate with Your design. Amen.

Practice

Pack a post-workout snack tonight for tomorrow's practice. Nuts, yogurt, or a shake. Eat within thirty minutes.

97
DYNAMIC WARM-UPS ALWAYS

"No discipline seems pleasant at the time, but painful. Later on, however, it produces a harvest of righteousness and peace for those who have been trained by it." Hebrews 12:11

Nobody in the Olympic warm-up area moved with more intention than Allyson Felix. While some sprinters bounced around casually, she performed a full dynamic warm-up routine: high knees, leg swings, walking lunges, arm circles, lateral shuffles. Every joint mobilized. Every muscle awakened. She treated it like the first event of the day, not a boring chore to rush through. After tearing her hamstring earlier in her career, she never skipped warm-ups again.   You have probably jogged a lazy lap and called it "warming up." Then halfway through practice, something tweaks and you are on the sideline icing your knee, confused. Research shows dynamic warm-ups reduce injury risk by 25% in youth athletes. That is one out of every four injuries just erased. Dynamic means movement: swinging your legs, rotating your hips, activating muscles before you demand everything from them. It feels annoying for five minutes. But those five minutes protect your entire season. Hebrews says discipline is painful now but produces a harvest later. Your warm-up is that harvest. Five minutes of intention saves five weeks on crutches.

Prayer

Lord, give me patience for the unglamorous habits that protect this body You gave me. Amen.

Practice

Learn a five-move dynamic warm-up routine this week. Do it before every single practice and game. No shortcuts.

98

COOL DOWN AND RECOVER

"I press on toward the goal to win the prize for which God has called me heavenward in Christ Jesus." Philippians 3:14

After crossing the finish line, after the cameras and cheers faded, Allyson Felix did something most athletes skip entirely. She cooled down. Static stretching, foam rolling, controlled breathing. While others grabbed their bags and rushed home, she spent ten to fifteen minutes gently stretching every major muscle group. Hamstrings held for thirty seconds. Quads. Hip flexors. Calves. She pressed on past the finish line because recovery was part of the race too.

Here is what happens when you skip the cool-down: your muscles stay shortened and tight, lactic acid pools in your legs, and tomorrow you wake up feeling like you aged forty years overnight. Static stretching after exercise improves flexibility and reduces next-day soreness significantly. Pressing on toward the goal does not mean sprinting 24/7. It means being smart enough to recover so you can sprint again tomorrow. God calls you heavenward, and the journey is long. You cannot finish if your body breaks down in chapter two. Ten minutes of stretching after practice is not weakness. It is wisdom wearing sweatpants.

Prayer

Jesus, teach me that slowing down after effort is not quitting. It is preparing for more. Amen.

Practice

After your next practice, stretch five major muscle groups for thirty seconds each. Set a timer. Do not skip it.

99

CORE OVER SHOW MUSCLES

"The bows of the warriors are broken, but those who stumbled are armed with strength." 1 Samuel 2:4

Allyson Felix never chased mirror muscles. While social media pushes teens toward bicep curls and chest presses for looks, Allyson spent hours on planks, dead bugs, bird dogs, and rotational core exercises. Her coaches knew that every athletic movement, sprinting, cutting, jumping, throwing, originates from the core. Your abs, obliques, lower back, and hips are the engine. Arms and chest are just the paint job. Her core stability let her maintain perfect sprint form when other runners fell apart in the final meters.

You have seen it happen. The kid who looks strongest in the mirror gets outrun, out-jumped, or falls apart in the clutch. That is because real athletic power comes from your center, not your selfie angles. A strong core improves balance, prevents back injuries, and transfers power to every limb. God told Samuel that warriors with impressive bows still break, but the stumbling ones armed with real strength rise. Build from the inside out. Twenty minutes of core work three times a week will change your game more than any arm curl ever could. Stop training for the mirror. Train for the moment.

Prayer

God, help me build strength that matters, from the inside out, in my body and my character. Amen.

Practice

Add a ten-minute core circuit to three practices this week. Planks, dead bugs, and side planks. Start today.

100
PREVENT THE INJURY

"Do you not know that your bodies are temples of the Holy Spirit, who is in you, whom you have received from God?" 1 Corinthians 6:19

When Nike dropped Allyson Felix for getting pregnant, she could have spiraled. Instead, she started her own shoe company, Saysh, and came back to win more Olympic medals as a mother. How? Because she had spent years protecting her body with injury prevention basics: proper sleep, balanced training loads, rest days, and listening to pain instead of ignoring it. She treated her body as a temple on loan from God, and that mindset kept her competing at the highest level for nearly twenty years.

You probably know someone who played through a "small" pain that became a season-ending injury. Youth athletes who train through warning signals suffer 60% more serious injuries. Your body talks to you. Sharp pain is a stop sign, not a suggestion. Soreness is normal. Stabbing, clicking, or swelling is not. Rest days are not lazy days; they are building days. God says your body is a temple of the Holy Spirit. You would not throw rocks at a church. So stop ignoring the signals your temple sends you. Rest when it whispers so it does not have to scream.

Prayer

Lord, help me respect the warning signs and rest without guilt. This temple is Yours. Amen.

Practice

Write down any pain you have been ignoring. Tell a coach or parent this week. Schedule one full rest day.

101
COOK 3 EASY MEALS

"At the end of the ten days they looked healthier and better nourished than any of the young men who ate the royal food." Daniel 1:15

Allyson Felix did not have a private chef for most of her career. She learned to prepare simple, clean meals herself. Scrambled eggs with spinach and toast for breakfast. Grilled chicken, rice, and vegetables for lunch. Overnight oats with fruit for a quick snack. Nothing fancy. Nothing expensive. Just real food she could make in fifteen minutes or less. She once said the simplest habit that separated her from other athletes was not a secret workout. It was knowing how to feed herself properly without depending on fast food drive-throughs.

Daniel refused the king's rich, processed royal food and chose vegetables, grains, and water. After ten days, he looked healthier than everyone else. You do not need a celebrity diet plan. You need three meals you can actually make. Research shows teens who prepare their own meals eat 40% more nutrients than those who rely on convenience food. Learn to scramble eggs. Learn to cook rice and season chicken. Learn to make overnight oats. Three meals. That is your starting lineup. When you control what goes into your body, you control what comes out of it on the field. Allyson proved it across five Olympics. Daniel proved it in a king's palace. Your turn starts in the kitchen tonight.

Prayer

God, give me the discipline of Daniel. Help me honor You with every meal I choose. Amen.

Practice

Pick one of these three meals: eggs and toast, chicken and rice, or overnight oats. Make it yourself this week.

WHAT WILL THEY REMEMBER?

One day your playing days will end.

Not someday far away. One actual day. You will walk off a field, a court, a track, a pool deck for the very last time. You might know it is your last game. You probably won't. The final whistle will blow, and the thing that filled your afternoons, your weekends, your entire identity will just quietly stop.

What happens then?

Here is what nobody will talk about. Your stats. Your trophy shelf. Your personal records. That highlight play you replayed a hundred times. Those things fade faster than you think. Trophies collect dust. Records get broken. Screenshots get buried.

But here is what people will never forget.

How you treated the teammate nobody else talked to. How you responded when the referee made a terrible call. How you showed up to practice on the days you wanted to quit. How you shook the opponent's hand after the worst loss of your life. How you pointed to heaven when the crowd was chanting your name. How you carried yourself when nobody was watching and when everybody was.

Kobe Bryant trained at 4 AM for 20 years, and the world remembers his discipline. Aaron Judge broke records clean in an era of shortcuts, and the world remembers his integrity. Allyson Felix got dropped by her sponsor for becoming a mother, came back, and won more Olympic medals than any American track athlete in history. The world remembers her resilience. Tim Tebow got cut from every NFL roster, never complained once, and built a foundation that has served thousands of children with special needs. The world remembers his heart.

None of those legacies are about stats.

Every single one is about character. And character is built by the small, invisible choices you make every single day. The 101 foundations in this book were never really about making you a better athlete. They were about making you a better human who happens to play a sport.

So here is your final challenge.

Do not try to master all 101. Not right now. Not this season. Pick three. Just three foundations that hit you the hardest while reading. The ones that made you stop and think, "That one is about me." Write them down somewhere you will see them every day. Your mirror. Your locker. The first page of your planner. Tell one person, a teammate, a parent, a coach, which three you picked. Spoken commitments become real commitments. Then start tomorrow. Not perfectly. Just faithfully.

One chapter told you to replace "I have to" with "I get to." One told you to celebrate your teammate's win like it was your own. One told you to show up on the days you don't feel like it. Whichever three you choose, they will change you. Not because the words are magic, but because God honors obedience in small things and turns them into big things you never saw coming.

And when doubt creeps back in, because it will, remember the ground rule you learned before the first chapter.

Your sport is what you do. It is never who you are.

You are a child of God. You were loved before your first practice and you will be loved long after your last game. Your worth was never on the scoreboard. It was settled at the cross. That is what makes you unstoppable. Not your speed, not your strength, not your skills. The unshakable, unchanging, never-running-out love of a God who made you on purpose, for a purpose.

A Closing Prayer for the Young Athlete and Their Family

God, thank You for the gift of competition, for the lessons hidden inside every win, every loss, and every ordinary Tuesday practice. Remind this young athlete that they are Yours first and always. Give them the courage to lead with faith, the humility to serve their teammates, and the resilience to get back up every single time life knocks them down. Bless the parents, coaches, and mentors walking beside them. Let this family be a light in every locker room, every bleacher section, and every conversation. We trust Your timing. We trust Your plan. We give You this athlete's entire journey, the trophies and the tears, and we believe You will do something beautiful with all of it. In Jesus' name, Amen.

The Final Truth

You were never meant to be unstoppable because of your talent. You are unstoppable because of whose you are.

"Act justly, love mercy, walk humbly with your God." Micah 6:8

Now go compete. The world is watching. But more importantly, he is watching. And He is already proud of you.

If you want to dive deeper:

If you loved these athlete stories and want to read even more true stories of sports heroes whose faith carried them through every trial, pick up Called to Be a Champion. It's full of powerful, real stories of athletes who walked with God through the toughest moments of their careers and came out stronger on the other side. It's the perfect next book for your UNSTOPPABLE journey.

A TRUE BLESSING!

If this book has encouraged you or helped you feel less alone, would you leave a quick review?

Even one sentence makes a huge difference and takes just a minute. As a small author, your feedback not only lifts my heart... it also helps other women of faith with find the support and hope they need.

Thank you for being part of this journey!

Scan this QR code with your phone to go to the review page and find this book.

Or

Go to your orders, find the book and click

"Write a product review"

Thank you <3